CHURCH GROWTH THROUGH
THE SUNDAY SCHOOL

John T. Sisemore

CHURCH GROWTH

Through the

SUNDAY SCHOOL

BROADMAN PRESS
Nashville, Tennessee

4262-37
ISBN: 0-8054-6237-6

Dewey Decimal Classification: 268
Subject headings: SUNDAY SCHOOLS / / CHURCH GROWTH
Library of Congress Catalog Card Number: 82-70870
Printed in the United States of America

Foreword

Although Jesus said: "I will build my church," God seems to always use human instrumentality in producing church growth. This observation does not mean that man alone can produce *authentic* church growth. Mere man lacks both the potential and the power to grow a church. Church growth is the product of a unique synergy—a coalescence of human effort and divine empowerment. "For it is God who works in you, inspiring both the will and the deed, for his own chosen purpose" (Phil. 2:13, NEB).

Church Growth Through the Sunday School speaks to both the human and the divine aspects of church growth. It features the key biblical concepts and the Sunday School dynamics which produce lasting church growth.

Although this book is concerned with the phenomenon of church growth, it does not relate particularly to the church growth movement, per se. However, it is clearly focused on the essential matters which the original church growth specialist— Jesus Christ—taught his followers about the subject.

Church Growth Through the Sunday School has a strong theological base. Church growth without a sound theology is much like a marriage without love—it is without real purpose. This book also reflects an educational bias. Biblical truth and Christian belief must be credibly stated in clear, factual, and logical propositions.

Church Growth Through the Sunday School speaks to all of the valid concerns about church growth. It is essentially an in-depth concept book. The *how-to* of church growth is included but the *what* and *why* of church growth are the essential concerns. This book is not a hastily prepared work designed to move quickly into an exciting field. Its roots are deeply embedded in a lifelong interest in building Sunday Schools and growing churches. It emerges from numerous successful growth experiences on the local church, state, and denominational levels. It was written while the author was teaching church growth in a noted seminary. Its concepts have been tested in the crucible of the classroom.

The basic purpose of *Church Growth Through the Sunday School* is to give biblical and practical guidance to churches that are trying to grow a Christ-centered, God-honoring church in a contemporary setting. To that end, it is sent forth in the name of him who said: "All authority in heaven and on earth has been given to me. You must therefore go and make the people of all nations my disciples. You must baptize them in the name of the Father and of the Son and of the Holy Spirit, and you must teach them to obey all the commands I have given you. And there is not a day when I will not be with you to the end of time" (Matt. 28:18-20, Barclay).

I Will Build My Church

"I will build my church," Jesus said,
   But he spoke not of steel and stone;
Nor of a place where saints could stay
   Shut off from their world, all alone.

"I will build my church," Jesus said,
   "No temple with steeple and spire;
But God's elect, his very own,
   His people whom I may inspire."

"I will build my church," Jesus said,
   "And give it a mission divine;
To go, to reach, to share my love,
   Making men of all nations mine."

"I will build my church," Jesus said,
   "To continue my work on earth;
To teach and preach the wondrous news
   Of new life through a second birth."

"I will build my church," Jesus said,
   And fill it with earnest desire;
To be my witness in the world,
   Set aglow by a sacred fire."

—John T. Sisemore

Contents

Part 1

The Key Concepts in Church Growth

1

A Total View of Church Growth

Growth is both the oldest experience and the most recent development in church life. On the surface this statement may seem to be a paradox. If so, it is a paradox of reality. It refers to the historical *fact* of unprecedented growth at Pentecost, and to the *hope* that the developing church growth movement will reclaim something of that original thrust which the early church experienced so profusely.

From the historical perspective, church growth seems to have had its beginning in a conversation between Jesus Christ and the apostle Peter. In response to Christ's probing question: "Who do men say that the Son of Man is?" Peter replied: "You are the Messiah, the Son of the living God." Jesus answered: "Simon son of Jonah, you are favoured indeed! You did not learn that from mortal man; it was revealed to you by the heavenly Father. And I say this to you: You are Peter, the Rock; and on this rock I will build my church" (Matt. 16:13,16-18, NEB). From this inauspicious interchange, church growth was set in motion. The details remain unknown, but by the time Jesus returned to the Heavenly Father there were about one hundred and twenty members of the Jerusalem church. Within ten days, at the Pentecost celebration, church growth took on landslide proportions. On that one day three thousand members were added to the church membership. Since that unprecedented experience, churches have grown, enlarged, expanded, multiplied, and

13

extended themselves from Jerusalem to every corner of the world.

In the contemporary setting church growth is becoming a worldwide phenomenon. Interestingly enough, the church growth movement itself is the outgrowth of another movement, the modern missionary movement. What is generally known as the Church Growth Movement had its beginning in a Third World mission field, India. Donald G. McGavran, a third-generation missionary, discovered the basic principles of church growth in his efforts to find better ways to plant new churches. The movement migrated to America in the early 1950s and is now ensconced in the School of World Mission at Fuller Theological Seminary, Pasadena, California.

The term *church growth* was used by McGavran to describe what he considered *mission* to be. His own definition of church growth is: "all that is involved in bringing men and women who do not have a personal relationship with Jesus Christ into fellowship with him and into responsible church membership." Although McGavran may not have intended it to be, his definition has three important dimensions: (1) church growth is adult-focused; (2) it is Christ-centered; and (3) it is church-oriented. By inference, at least, the definition is also largely concerned with the numerical growth of a church.

Although the church growth movement seems to recognize the larger dimensions of church growth, the basic interest of the movement is directed toward the evangelistic activities which are associated with quantitative growth. Without doubt the matter of making disciples is the major emphasis that every church growth effort must pursue. Nevertheless, the New Testament gives full attention to a *total* view of church growth. There are evidences of concern to be found all through the New Testament which include the matter of balance in the various areas of growth. These more inclusive views of growth need to be reflected in all church growth plans and programs.

Authentic church growth is a very complex and intricate

matter. There are numerous factors involved, so much so, that it is difficult to separate the various parts from the whole. The interrelatedness of the several factors is further complicated by the human tendency to give priority to only one aspect of growth. What is desperately needed is a holistic view of growth. From this viewpoint there is a confluence of all of the areas of growth into a living whole. In the holistic view, each one of the parts makes its best contribution to the whole when it is blended into a balanced approach to growth. When the separate aspects of church growth are viewed individually, they seem to be *sequences* rather than *priorities*. However, even in a sequential concept of growth there is no fixed pattern or chronology. In fact, different churches seem to need differing sequences at any given time and even in the same church the growth sequences seem to change from time to time. The inescapable conclusion is that all areas of church growth are important and are needed in some way all at the same time. This need speaks to the matter of balance. It is also true that a balanced approach to growth does not mean that every aspect of growth should receive the same attention or the same emphasis all of the time. Such an approach would be equal emphasis, not balanced emphasis.

Some seven basic areas of church growth need to claim the attention of a church. These aspects of growth are not all of equal significance but together they provide an opportunity of immense significance and challenge.

1. Growth in the Number of Believers

All of the New Testament churches differed dramatically in their individual growth patterns. Nevertheless, there was one common element in each growth experience. The numerical growth of the church body was the most visible and probably the most significant characteristic of each church. The Book of Acts carefully records these statistical achievements. Luke's purpose in writing Acts was apparently to record growth and then validate the subsequent separation of Christianity from its roots in Judaism. These accounts give special attention to the separation from the racial, national, and religious legalism which characterized Judaism. In the process of recording this history of growth and separation, Luke left a marvelous account of several epochs in church growth. These epochs capsuled here portray a series of phenomenal church growth experiences and conclude with a summary statement regarding the numerical growth of the churches.

(1) Growth of the Jerusalem Church (Acts 1:1 to 6:7)

This first section of Acts presents Christianity in a unique setting. The church at Jerusalem was entirely Jewish. Likely some proselytes were included, but they were previous converts to Judaism who had become Christians. The Jerusalem church had the most astounding growth experience of all time. The summary statement of the Acts account is found in Acts 6:7. It indicates that (1) the gospel spread rapidly, (2) the disciples multiplied greatly, and (3) the Jewish priests obeyed openly.

(2) Growth in Palestine and Samaria (Acts 6:8 to 9:31)

The second period of church growth was in effect a spillover from Jerusalem and the first church there. As the gospel began to spread, it arrived in Judea, Galilee, and Samaria. Two very significant events introduced a cause-and-effect motivation for growth. These events were the slaying of Stephen and the conversion of Saul of Tarsus. Luke's summary of this period highlights the geographical expansion of the church. His report says: "Meanwhile the church, throughout Judaea, Galilee, and Samaria, was left in peace to build up its strength. In the fear of the Lord, upheld by the Holy Spirit, it held on its way and grew in numbers" (Acts 9:31, NEB).

(3) Growth in Gentile Lands (Acts 9:32 to 12:24)

The third epoch of growth recorded in the Book of Acts is one which involved the removal of racial barriers to the gospel. Already Christianity had moved across religious and geographical frontiers, and now it faced the most formidable obstruction of all, racial prejudice. Although Philip had scaled the racial wall when he helped the Ethiopian eunuch come to Christ, the church was still largely Jewish and the Gentile world was not even considered an acceptable candidate for the gospel. When Peter went to Samaria to investigate the conversion of the hated half-breeds, he became convinced that the gospel was for non-Jews also. Later, his encounter with Cornelius further assured him that Christianity was a universal religion.

During this period of interracial growth of the church, Barnabas was sent by the Jerusalem church to study the new church that was developing in Antioch of Syria. He learned that some of the Jews who had fled for their lives from Jerusalem had been preaching the gospel in Phoenicia, Cyprus, and Antioch. In Antioch some of the believers began to share the gospel with the Greeks. The result was overwhelming, for the Gentiles turned to Christ in great numbers. A new church was the result. It was at Antioch, in this very church where believers were first called the Christ-people, Christians. It was also from this church that the thrust of the gospel went out to the Gentile world.

This period of church growth was a turbulent time of transition. Famine overtook the Jerusalem church. Persecution was intense. And the gospel was moving in unexpected ways and into unprecedented acceptance by non-Jews. The growth of the church in Gentile lands and in non-Jewish cultures was difficult for many of the Jerusalem Christians to accept. Luke's summary of church growth at the end of this section is a classic case of understatement: "The word of God grew and multiplied" (Acts 12:24). The word *multiplied* is a significantly different change from his usual use of the word *added*. Growth was so great that exact numbers could no longer be given!

(4) Growth Through a Missionary Movement
(Acts 12:25 to 16:5)

The fourth great epoch in church growth portrays a time of dramatic change. The Jerusalem church held its place of prominence, but it lost its leadership role in Christianity. The loss of leadership was a result of the inability of the Jewish Christians to accept as brothers the new Gentile converts.

At the same time the church in Antioch was demonstrating to the world that Gentiles made commendable Christians. They not only accepted all who responded to the gospel, but they went to all lengths to see that everyone heard the gospel. These facts make this period of church growth seem to be both a tragedy and a triumph. It was tragic because the Jewish Christians began out of prejudice to exclude themselves. It was triumphant because the Gentiles turned to Christ in ever-increasing numbers.

When Paul and Barnabas set out to the north and west to preach to the Jews, they met with resistance and resentment. In the wake of Jewish rejection they turned to the Gentiles. This act opened up the missionary movement of the gospel and, in effect, Christianity crossed over racial lines to become the religion of the Gentile world. At this point the conquest of the Greco-Roman world became the target of Christianity. The burgeoning growth of the Antioch church was duplicated again and again throughout Galatia, Asia Minor, and eventually through the civilized world.

Paul must have suffered immensely from the rejection of the Jews, but there is no hint of it in the crisp report of this phase of growth. Luke, always the positive reporter, simply said: "And so, day by day, the congregations grew stronger in faith and increased in number" (Acts 16:5, NEB).

(5) Growth in the Urban Centers (Acts 16:6 to 19:20)

This epoch is a drama of the cities. There is a decided shift in focus to church extension. The great population centers of the Western world became the outreach targets of Christian missions. Not only did the gospel thrust move from a Jewish context to a Gentile context, but it also moved from the Eastern world to the Western world. Great cities such as Philippi, Thessalonica,

Berea, Athens, Corinth, and Ephesus became the centers of Christian missions. Luke's summary of the new ways for the New Way is guardedly optimistic: "The word of the Lord showed its power, spreading more and more widely and effectively" (Acts 19:20, NEB).

(6) Growth in the Roman Empire (Acts 19:21 to 28:31)

The final epoch of church growth could be titled "Operation Rome." For a long time Paul had wanted to preach the gospel in Rome. It was a major goal, if not a specific strategy. Even though Paul was imprisoned, he realized his goal and he preached Christ to all who came near him.

This phase of church growth is nothing short of a miracle of God's grace. The Word of God, the gospel of Jesus Christ, and the growth of the church came to a glorious climax in Paul's arrival in Rome. Every barrier known to man had been experienced, and in every case triumph had come. The barriers of a national religion, a racial impactment, geographical boundaries, political resistance, and internal strife were all swallowed up in the freedom of the gospel. The church always marched on. The final report from Luke says: "And he [Paul] lived there two whole years at his own expense, and welcomed all who came to him, preaching the kingdom of God and teaching the Lord Jesus Christ quite openly and unhindered" (Acts 28:30-31, RSV). The church had met and faced all hindrances, and in the end it marched on *unhindered*.

These six epochs of church growth constitute an inspired record of what an authentic church can achieve when its only concern is the unreached multitudes. It is noteworthy that there are at least nineteen clear references to church growth found in the Book of Acts. This abundance of data regarding growth makes it clear that there is a divine concern for the growth of a church. Furthermore, it seems clear that both the continuing existence of a church and the future of Christianity itself are solidly embedded in a strong, healthy growth pattern. Moreover, as long as there are any unsaved persons within reach of a given church, that church is under divine obligation to do everything possible to bring those persons to Christ and into responsible church membership. Failure at this point is to violate the Great Commission and to prostitute the nature of the church. A positive attitude toward growth and a compassionate concern for persons are the keys to church growth. But more than that, they are the evidence of an authentic church of Jesus Christ.

2. Growth in the Maturity of the Church Members

In spite of the fact that the New Testament churches were growth-oriented, and actually seemed to give their entire energies to making disciples, they found time for the spiritual growth of the members. Apparently a strong commitment to outreach did not keep them from being quality minded. In fact, there seems to be a very strong relationship between the excitement of reaching more people and developing an in-depth quality of spiritual mindedness. At any rate, the early churches, especially the Jerusalem church, had an inner reserve of spiritual power that emerged as a fresh source of courage and effectiveness in their growth activities.

A clue to the relationship between inner strength and outer ability is found in the brief statement in Acts 2:42. The *New English Bible* translates the verse this way: "They met constantly to hear the apostles teach, and to share the common life, to break bread, and to pray." This verse is only a part of a larger passage which delineates the essential characteristics of a spiritually mature church. However, this verse is the essence of what creates a spiritual church and grows mature church members. The passage quoted previously portrays a unique form of fellowship. It is not just a picture of good friends who are involved in an exciting activity. It is a *koinonia* of the Spirit. It is a group of reborn persons who have become one in Christ. They not only had a feeling of unity, they were also experiencing both a vertical relationship with God and a resultant horizontal relationship with each other as brothers and sisters in Christ. They were caught up in a mutuality of love that belongs only to those who are in spiritual union with Jesus Christ. There were three highly distinctive aspects of fellowship in that *koinonia*.

(1) *It was a learning fellowship.*—The quality of the dynamics that these early believers were experiencing is all but unknown to contemporary Christians. They had a deep and intensive desire to know not only the Scriptures but to also understand how the apostles related them to Jesus Christ. The fact that all of the persons had been saved in adulthood probably accounts for the deep interest which bound them together. They knew by recent experience what it meant to be a Christian. They were eager to learn more about the new life that was so exciting and rewarding. Undoubtedly more present-day churches would experience this same kind of joyful excitement if they were constantly winning unsaved adults and involving them in Bible study. This inflow of freshness in the life of a church is probably the most significant aspect of spiritual growth both on the part of the individuals involved and the church as a body of Christ.

There are several Greek words used in the Scriptures to describe the kind of teaching done in the early churches. The most commonly used word is *didasko.* It refers to the teaching of both unsaved persons and new converts. The word is not concerned with the methodology or even the teaching-learning process. It is concerned with the content of the truth that was taught. It refers to the kind of teaching which strengthened the faith of the saved and resulted in the edification of the church. Bible teaching is the major factor in spiritual growth and the undergirding factor in church fellowship. Furthermore, the right kind of Bible teaching is the finest outreach asset a church can have.

(2) *It was a relating fellowship.*—Spiritual growth on the part of church members is greatly enhanced by the relations within the church. Relationships which develop *authentic Christian maturity* are those that are experienced while serving God

within the fellowship of a church. The early Christians knew nothing about a "churchless" Christianity. They were immediately added to the churches, and they were steadfast in their devotion to the fellowship. John pointed out the significance of relational Christianity when he wrote: "We proclaim to you what we have seen and heard, so that you also may have fellowship with us. And our fellowship is with the Father and with his Son, Jesus Christ" (1 John 1:3, NIV).

Breaking bread together and praying are the two vital experiences which Luke mentioned in Acts 2:42. These two activities refresh the body and invigorate the spirit. When they are experienced in a setting of mutual love and acceptance, they have a reciprocal effect. They enhance each other and enrich all relationships. Unfortunately, the church at Corinth went to excess in eating together, and problems developed. Yet, the "religious meal" had both a pagan and Jewish background. It may have been a necessity for survival in the Jerusalem church, but it proved to be a blessing and an invaluable part of the experiences of the church. Luke records the fact that these fellowship meals added greatly to the vitality of the church fellowship: "And day by day, attending the temple together and breaking bread in their homes, they partook of food with glad and generous hearts, praising God and having favor with all the people" (Acts 2:46-47, RSV).

(3) *It was a praying fellowship.*—Prayer was such an indispensable part of the early church life that it would be easy to assume that it was almost the only important aspect of fellowship. Many, if not most, of the references to prayer in the New Testament are found in the context of the corporate life of the church. Prayer is no doubt the best way for a church to be together, to get together, and to stay together. It is in prayer that a church discerns the will of God for the church. It is in prayer that a church finds that seeking a consensus, arriving at a compromise, or letting the majority rule is unnecessary. Prayer becomes the context in which a church discovers that God has a

will for every question and that finding that will is a most valuable part of the relationship between Christians.

As far as Christians are concerned, prayer is a natural expression of their common relationship to God through Christ. They pray together because they have common needs, common interests, and common aspirations. Just as social fulfillment is found in companionship with friends, so is spiritual *koinonia* found in prayer with trusted and faithful members of a church.

3. Growth in the Strength of the Church

A vital spirituality is not only necessary to the members of a church, it is also essential to the very being of a church. This statement does not mean that a church cannot exist as an *institution* without being mature, but it does mean that a church cannot exist as a *maturing organism* unless it is being built up in the faith.

Paul spoke to the matter of spiritual vitality on many occasions. He referred to it as edification, or the building up of the body of Christ, the local church. Paul also gave special instructions about the standards by which church strength can be measured. The basic passage which speaks to church maturity and strength is Ephesians 4:13-32. In this passage a number of evidences of maturity are presented. Here is at least a partial listing:

(1) A oneness of faith which was expressed in a sense of unity;

(2) A comprehension of what is known about God's Son;

(3) A level of maturity that compares favorably with the completeness (perfection) found in Christ;

(4) A doctrinal stability which is able to withstand erroneous teaching;

(5) A way of church life which lovingly expresses truth;

(6) A continuing experience of growth in Christ;

(7) A church body which functions cooperatively and is constantly building up itself in Christian love;

(8) A life-style which is learned from Christ;

(9) A continual renewing of the mind and spirit;

(10) A rejection of all that is false and untrue;

(11) An ability to handle anger positively;

(12) A membership which makes a living in an honorable way;

(13) A manner of communication that is clean and wholesome;

(14) An earnest effort to avoid grieving the Holy Spirit;

(15) An avoidance of intemperate attitudes and relationships;

(16) A helpful and compassionate attitude toward all other members of the church family.

Paul frequently expressed his concern for a spiritually mature church. He used three words to serve as goals and standards: (1) *faith*, (2) *hope*, and (3) *love*. He used these words to characterize mature Christians and to refer to strong churches. The entire process of personal growth was related to the process of edification of the church. As individual Christians grow toward Christlikeness, they become mature; and as they become mature, the church becomes complete in Christ. Beyond any doubt there is a very strong correlation between growing Christians and maturing churches. The special spiritual dimension that is so essential to a Christian is carried over into all of the qualities of the church body. There is an inextricable relationship between the growth of persons and the growth of the body of Christ.

Presently, as in New Testament times, it is easy for some Christians to confuse spiritual maturity with manifestations of spiritual gifts. It should be understood that the possession of spiritual gifts is not the same thing as spiritual maturity. The church at Corinth had more spiritual gifts and more apparent spiritual manifestations than any other New Testament church. But this church also had more immaturity and spiritual destitution than any other church. Amid the many implications of these two seemingly contradictory facts, there is ample evidence that spiritual maturity is far more than manifestations of any kind, and not at all the same as spiritual gifts for the service of God. It is also clear that the spiritual growth of Christians and the maturity of a church do not depend on spiritual gifts or manifestations but on the quality of love and concern which the members have for each other. See 1 Thessalonians 3:12 for further study of this concept.

The Book of Acts carefully records the numerical growth of the early churches, but it also faithfully catalogs the spiritual growth of the churches as well. In spite of this fact, many persons get caught up in defending either quantitative or qualitative growth to the exclusion of the other. This is a futile if not a foolish effort. Quantity and quality are not opposites; neither are they an *either/or* proposition. These two aspects of church growth are *both/and* concepts. It is essential that a church grow both numerically *and* spiritually. As a matter of fact, both of these aspects are only part of a greater concern, making disciples. The quantitative and qualitative aspects of growth are simply two ways of making disciples.

When the emphasis is placed on church *growth*, the focus is on outreach to new people and the result is numerical growth. When the emphasis is on *church* growth, the focus is on spiritual maturation and the result is the edification of the church. Both of these growth experiences are inherent in the nature of a church. They are mutually complementary and supplementary. Each one causes the other to occur. The absence of either one causes the other to become ineffective. Any long-term deficiency in either numerical growth or spiritual growth will result in the eventual decline and possible death of a church. When a church is spiritually vital, it will in all probability enjoy a healthy growth pattern. Likewise, when a church fails to reach more people, it is or has been in a declining state for an extended period of time. To be sure, a facade for either type of growth will likely be in evidence.

For example, a spiritually deficient church may *appear* to be growing because of the transfer of members from other churches. Or, it may seem to be growing simply by evangelizing the children of the members. Underneath it all, there will be few new people coming into the church by the new birth. Conversely, the nongrowing church may appear to be spiritually vital because of a hyperactivity syndrome. The revealing sign, however, is an introverted fellowship which has little concern for the unreached persons in the community.

In the final analysis, the only defensible question about numerical and spiritual growth is whether they are both occurring at a continuing level appropriate to the potential.

4. Growth in the Influence of the Church

It is little short of a tragedy when a church has no more influence on a community than to add an edifice to the landscape. The tragedy is compounded when it is recalled that a church is itself a community—a community of believers—planted by God in a larger community which desperately needs the influence of the saved community.

Churches often fail to make an appreciable impact on their community simply because the members see their buildings as the only link to the community. In such cases the church buildings become little more than a hideaway for the faithful few to gather for worship. Without question worship is important, and a building that is conducive to worship is quite desirable. However, the attendance of the members and their worship together exert very little influence on the community. An authentic church must do much more than attend services if it is to make an obvious difference in a community.

Real influence begins with the realization that the nature and purpose of a church requires a church to gather so that it may scatter to do its work. The New Testament churches had no buildings in which to worship or to work. They were forced onto the streets and into the open places. It was in those public areas that they became influential in the community, state, and world. Contemporary churches must find and use effectively the best approaches to community influence. Granted, some communities are either indifferent to, or unfriendly toward churches;

nevertheless, every church needs to accept the fact that its local community is its primary and special field of effort. Moreover, a church should not forget that its own community needs a strong spiritual influence from the church more than it needs anything else.

A church exists to bring persons to God through Jesus Christ. Growing out of this unique assignment are many concomitant influences on society in general and on the local community in particular. For example, a church should have an influence on the ethics of a community. It should have a wholesome impact on the social life of the community. It should lift the moral level of the community. And, ultimately, a church should improve the life-style of the community.

These influences are not the result of programmed approaches to community betterment. They are indirect and sometimes incidental outcomes because they are normal results of making disciples. These community influences occur primarily because church members grow, because the church is strengthened, and because the institutional life of the church creates a better sense of community life.

Every aspect of society is strengthened when God's people work at applying biblical truths and principles, when they hold to and lift up moral values, and when they live righteously in all of their relationships in the community. Being a helpful and responsible citizen wields a strong personal and corporate influence on a community. Honorable citizenship is an easily-read lesson in turning spiritual ideals into practical realities.

Spiritual influence cannot be forced on a community. When this approach is used, a church becomes manipulatory, if not a controlling pressure on the community. Christianity is an outgoing, loving, and supporting religion that is motivated by the love of Christ. It is not a political force which seeks to coerce or control. Influence is not a matter of social action or psychological management of people. Influence that is genuinely spiritual is a product of compassion. It is an achievement of growing Christians who by their own example of moral living, ethical dealings, and honorable practices provide the "salt of the earth" and "the light of the world."

5. Growth in the Functional Ability of the Church

A church is a living, growing, functioning organism. Because it is an organism, and especially because it is a living body of Christ, a church must function in a sound and healthy manner. The functional life of a church requires adequate organization and effective administration. Otherwise, it is not a healthy organism. It will, at best, be weak and ineffective.

Like any other organism, a church can become so engrossed in the process of maintaining its existence that it lives for no other purpose. However, this possibility does not justify a church in neglecting its functional needs, neither does it justify a disdain for organization and administration. The functional needs of a church are essential to every aspect of its growth and ministry. Good organization and effective administration are in every way superior to an incompetent or laissez-faire approach to existence. The Lord's work deserves more than the casual approach to the functions of the body. It deserves careful and competent attention at all times. Neither an excessive desire for efficiency nor a total disregard for good work makes any spiritual contribution to a church. On the other hand, both of these attitudes will have a pronounced effect on the spiritual health of a church.

While it is true that in some situations structural and organizational efficiency seems to become an end rather than a means, it is also true that the lack of such efficiency is a very serious handicap to many churches. Actually the requirements of the Great Commission make necessary such things as organization, administration, and even maintenance care. These factors are required in making and growing disciples of Jesus Christ. They are not insignificant details; rather they are means to obedience.

A growing church will by necessity have to adjust, enlarge,

and restructure its organization periodically, especially its Sunday School organization. At intervals it will be necessary to adopt new organizational patterns and even new forms of structure. The dynamics of a growing Sunday School cannot be maintained with the same organizational structure year by year. Growth introduces new dynamics which must be administered creatively or growth will be inhibited simply because the organizational pattern will not support more growth.

These observations lay the groundwork for a rather obvious conclusion: *flexibility* in the outreach, educational, and administrative functions is made necessary by church growth. Conversely, flexibility supports and promotes church growth. The ability of a church to make these functional adjustments will to a very large degree determine both the growth and progress of the church. Commitment to past approaches on the grounds that "we have always done it this way" is a sure sign of degenerate "rutualism." On the other hand, the ability of a church to adjust as needed will keep the church from becoming stymied in its progress and petrified in its present state. A church or a Sunday School that becomes concerned about preserving its heritage more than about making new history is becoming institutionalized. It has reached the point of making its institutional functions the end rather than the means. A church must function effectively, but a maintenance mentality is disaster in disguise.

6. Growth in the Quality of Church Ministries

In a very real sense a church is the functional body of Jesus Christ. It is God's agency through which he continues to minister to the needs of people, especially the redemptive needs of the world. When Jesus spoke to the apostles before his departure to be with the Father, he said: "Peace! Just as the Father has commissioned me, so I am sending you forth" (author's translation of John 20:21). Not only has the church been given the Great Commission, but it also has received by transfer

Christ's own personal commission from the Father.

The methods by which a church carries out the representative acts of Christ are known as ministries. These ministries may be defined in various ways and be identified by various terms; however, all the terms take on the essence of ministry. Ministry is an appropriate term because Christians are in every respect the ministers of Jesus Christ. As his emissaries they are to do what he did while on earth. Almost all of the things which Jesus did are wrapped up in three terms: (1) teaching, (2) preaching, and (3) ministering to human need. These things are still the heart of the work of a church, the tasks of a Sunday School, and the basis of personal Christian ministry. In a very real sense these are the things a church must do to communicate the gospel of Christ. Also, there is a very strong correlation between these activities that is evident in several ways. For example, the gospel requires communication. Communication is best achieved through teaching and preaching. Also, teaching and preaching undergird compassion. Likewise compassion generates concern for human need and leads to efforts to relieve need. Each of these ministries interlocks with the others, and yet they are all individually unique and specific areas of Christian ministry. All of the ministries are both church or corporate ministries, as well as personal ministries of Christians.

There is a very distinctive value or quality feature to ministry both on the personal level and the church level. This qualitative vein was experienced by the apostles when they attempted to heal the lunatic. They failed to heal the man because they had a defective faith. It was necessary that they possess a deeper level of faith (Matt. 17:14-20). The quality of their faith improved for it is reported that at a later time even the devils were obedient to them. Their ability to minister became improved qualitatively.

The possibility of growth in one's ability to minister is illustrated in Paul's special instructions to Timothy. Paul explained to Timothy how he should improve. (See 2 Tim. 2.)

On the corporate or church level, the quality of ministry must constantly be improved. The reason is that improvement in the quality of ministry is directly related to growth. To put it another way, many churches do not grow simply because their ministries are performed in a submarginal manner. The apostle Paul spoke to the matter of quality when he wrote these words to Timothy: "Study to shew thyself approved unto God, a workman that needeth not to be ashamed, rightly dividing the word of truth" (2 Tim. 2:15). This passage implies that a better quality of ministry is more than a human performance matter. It is an obligation involved in the nature of ministry because ministry is man representing God. The manner in which a person ministers either limits or facilitates God's own work through man. The quality of this man-for-God-to-man activity bears a strong influence on growth. It can well be the difference between a flourishing church or a floundering one.

7. Growth in the Regions Beyond

Genuine church growth cannot be contained. It is a phenomenon that leaps over all barriers and crosses all lines of demarcation. For example, when Philip reached out to the Ethiopian eunuch, he moved across both racial lines and religious classifications. That same event cracked open the solid wall of partition that had so long kept Jews and Gentiles alienated. Although Judaism had many proselytes, it was still a religion based on racial lines. The conversion of the eunuch threw open the floodgates, and Christianity began spilling over into all of the surrounding nations. Although there were some difficult times, the thrust of Christianity moved from country to country. In this process of geographical growth the center of Christianity moved from Jerusalem to Antioch and from Jewish domination to Gentile ascendancy. As the gospel spread from area to area, cultures met and clashed. Yet each eventually became a viable expression of the freedom that is in Christ and the fellowship that knows no boundaries because it belongs to the church.

This small capsule of church growth in its geographical expression portrays the church as an *expanding* organism. It is an organism that expands in an ever-widening circle. In this growth pattern it enlarges locally, it expands culturally, it extends geographically, and it multiplies internationally. Its growth pattern moves constantly and dynamically to the regions beyond.

Although some congregations are born, flourish, and die, other churches arise to keep the gospel spreading and the number of disciples multiplying. In the process some congregations succumb to the impact of social change. Others adjust and overcome the adverse effect of radical change. Also, some congregations seem to have more human qualities than spiritual qualities and thereby stagnate. Conversely, other churches are reborn so that they become spiritual lighthouses in hostile environments.

All of these variables between churches point to a certain transcendent quality about the church. It has an expansive tendency that cannot be denied. A church *must* grow—that is its nature. A church *must* grow—that is its mission. A church *must* grow—that is its motivation. And, because of this innate urge to grow, a church *can* grow in any environment, in any culture, in any civilization.

An authentic, healthy church grows in all the dimensions included in this *total view* of church growth. On the other hand, a church which fails to grow is showing signs of being or becoming unhealthy. If a church does not want to grow, or if, in fact, it refuses to grow, it is showing its counterfeit nature and revealing its death wish. The fact is inescapable—a church *must* grow because growth is the only authenticating factor for a church. A church is a *genuine* church if it grows. A church is *apocryphal* if it fails to grow.

In some ways these statements may seem harsh or judgmental. Nevertheless, they are accurate. The church was *born* in a growth context; the church was *commissioned* with a growth assignment; the church was *launched* with a growth promise; the church was *inaugurated* with a growth experience; and the church was *authenticated* by a growth record. A *church* grows!

2

A Biblical Foundation for Church Growth

One of the most basic Christian beliefs is the fact that the Bible is God's inspired Word. As such, it is a book of total integrity, having authority in all matters of religion. Among other things, this concept means that the Bible is the guide to God's will concerning the interests and activities of a church. Stated as a principle, this doctrine alleges that *every activity of a church must have a solid biblical base if it is to be a valid church practice.* Manifestly, this principle must be applied to the matter of growth as well as to all other church concerns. Therefore, if growth is to be an authentic concern of a church, it must have a biblical foundation that is neither forced nor superimposed.

Does the Bible have anything to say about church growth? Do the Scriptures command, or even imply, that a church should grow? Are there any examples of church growth found in the Scriptures? Is the idea of church growth biblically valid?

In speaking about Christ's relation to the church, Paul said: "For it is under His [Christ's] direction that the whole body is perfectly adjusted and united by every joint that furnishes its supplies; and so by the proper functioning of each particular part there is brought about *a growing of the body for its building up in love*" (Eph. 4:16, author's italics). This translation by Charles B. Williams affirms healthy church growth. The Bible also speaks about several other types of church growth as well. Yet the term *church growth* does not occur in the Bible, nor is there

33

any reference to a specific growth movement. Nevertheless, both the *concept* of church growth and the *fact* of church growth are amply supported by the Scriptures. As a matter of fact, the biblical coverage of church growth is so extensive it would require an entire book to do justice to the concept. The Book of Acts alone records some nineteen growth experiences, and there are numerous references to growth in other biblical accounts. Some seven of these growth perspectives are presented herewith.

1. Church Growth Is Embedded in the Divine Purpose

Every religion, including Christianity, has several things in common. For example: All religions have some type of deity, one or more devout leaders, at least one hallowed place, a sacred book, some principles for daily life, a special community of adherents, induction rites into membership, and a plan of propagation. However, there is one unique distinction between Christianity and the religions of the world. In all of the other religions, *man is seen in a search for God.* In Christianity, the very reverse is true: *God is always seeking man.* The Almighty God of the Old Testament is portrayed as the seeking Heavenly Father in the New Testament. It is the essence of God's nature to seek his erring creatures. In the Old Testament he offers mercy and pardon: "Ho, every one that thirsteth, come ye to the waters, and he that hath no money; come ye, buy, and eat; yea, come, buy wine and milk without money and without price" (Isa. 55:1). In the New Testament, God is the provider of salvation: "But God commendeth his love toward us, in that, while we were yet sinners, Christ died for us" (Rom. 5:8). Bringing men to himself through Christ is the essence of God's eternal purpose.

The Scriptures teach that God acting as a seeking, yearning, Heavenly Father, has been at work on behalf of a disobedient and unredeemed world ever since Adam and Eve transgressed God's will and plunged humanity into dreadful sin. God's redemptive purpose was first revealed in his call to Abraham. That purpose was demonstrated in his mighty acts of deliverance for Israel. God's purpose was supremely manifest when he gave his only Son as a remedy for the sins of the world. God's purpose was at work when Jesus came as the compassionate Savior "to seek and to save that which was lost" (Luke 19:10). This same divine purpose was the motivation involved in God's creation of a new people for himself "a chosen generation, a royal priesthood, an holy nation, a peculiar people" (1 Pet. 2:9a). This new people, as God's "private possession" (peculiar), was gathered into a new *ekklesia*, his church.

As individuals respond to Christ's love through the prompting of the Holy Spirit, the divine purpose is being realized. The outcome of this divine activity is the salvation of "whosoever will." Church growth is the inevitable result of this divine enterprise. In the process of reconciling his alienated creation, God fulfills his heart's desire, authenticates Christ's magnificent sacrifice, and calls into a spiritual community those who can serve as agents of reconciliation. In each of these supernatural actions God is expanding his redemptive work throughout the world, calling out a people unto himself, and enlarging the body of Christ. In the light of these significant events it becomes obvious to all that it is God's immutable intent, his holy will, and his divine purpose to help his churches grow.

2. Growth Is Inherent in the Nature of a Church

When Jesus said: "I will build my church; and the gates of hell shall not prevail against it" (Matt. 16:18), he revealed a divine plan that had been in existence since the beginning. It was a unique plan conceived in the mind of God. It was to be implemented by the Son of God. It was to be empowered by the Spirit of God. God's plan was to create "the church of the living God" (1 Tim. 3:15). It was to be made up of living persons who had been redeemed and were being perfected by his grace.

The word *church* (*ekklesia*) was a very familiar word to first-century people. Any group that had been "called out" or assembled for a special purpose was an *ekklesia*. However, the *ekklesia* of Jesus Christ had a whole new dimension of meaning. His *ekklesia* was to be made up of *persons who had been reborn.* This *ekklesia* was to be a unique relationship of baptized believers. It was to be *a family of God* because all of the members were to be related to Christ. This family would become a local "body of Christ" (Rom. 12:5) which would live to do the will of God. *Christ's ekklesia was to be a living, growing, developing, reproducing organism with a spiritual nature and a human manifestation.*

As a spiritual organism a church must function in harmony with its nature. If its nature is to grow—and it is—all of its functions must be growth related and growth producing. To function in any other way would be to violate its nature and to corrupt its purpose. To become caught up in activities that are not essential to growth, or in harmony with its growth potential, a church would forfeit its right to be a church. To continue to function in nongrowth ways would mean the eventual loss of identity as a church even if it continued to survive as a congregation. Any church which decides to function as a *self-serving institution* no longer reflects the uniqueness of a body of Christ.

For a church, as in all other organisms, the *body* is the medium of expression. It is through the *body* that the organism expresses its nature and fulfills its normal functions. As a "body of Christ," a church must function as Christ's human body. This means that a church must express the nature of Christ and function in the same manner in which he functioned while he was on earth. It is also imperative that a church "bring men to God through Jesus Christ" for this is the way in which the body reproduces itself. If a church turns away from these significant functions to serve itself, and the personal needs of its members, it will be unable to achieve its divine objectives thereby casting doubt on its authenticity and bringing shame to its founder.

The first church in Jerusalem set a marvelous pattern and high-level standard of growth. At times it seemed to have no purpose other than its outreach and evangelistic efforts. Its interests all appeared to be directed toward reaching people for Christ. Undoubtedly all of the early churches were growing churches. They understood that their mission was to bring more and more people to Christ and into membership in his body. These churches grew because it was their *nature to grow*. They grew because it was the very *essence of their being*. Growth was the creative force and the controlling factor in all that they did. Their total commitment to their purpose was the cause of their unique mark on Christian history.

These growth characteristics of the early churches can be interpreted to mean only one thing: they were *genuine* churches. They justified their existence. They *were* what they were supposed to *be*. They were functioning, healthy, spiritual organisms. These churches earned the right to be called a church. They were the reflection of the compassionate heart and the untiring spirit of Christ.

Saul of Tarsus tried desperately to destroy the first church—until he met Christ on the road to Damascus. After that life-changing experience he did more than any other person to plant churches, strengthen their outreach, and work for their growth. This unique turn of events demonstrated what one genuine Christian can do to help a church *be* a church.

Church growth is not some upbeat movement to revive a decadent institution. It is a fresh realization that a church is supernatural in origin and is the body of Jesus Christ on earth. As such, its very nature is to grow. And when a church does grow, it demonstrates its loyalty to Christ and its faithfulness to his singular purpose. Likewise, when a church fails to grow, it is not conscientiously representing the one who "loved the church, and gave himself for it" (Eph. 5:25b).

3. Growth Is Produced by God

God alone can produce authentic church growth. This kind of growth is never a mere accident of fortuitous circumstances. Churches do not grow because of favorable situations, unusual and talented leadership, or even from exceptional preaching and teaching of the gospel. They grow for one simple reason—*God wants them to grow.* But church growth is not an end in itself. It is a result of something even more important: the salvation of persons. God is "not willing that any should perish, but that all should come to repentance" (2 Pet. 3:9*b*). Growth is the evidence of God at work.

From the very beginning of the church, growth has been a matter of divine initiative. During those so-called "silent years" in the ministry of Jesus, he was in reality laying the foundations for church growth. He was, in effect, growing his church when he called the apostles. He was growing his church when he gathered about him responsive men and women to be his followers. He was growing his church when he "went about doing good" (Acts 10:38*b*). He was growing his church when he taught the people. He was growing his church when he preached to the multitudes. He was growing his church when he ministered to the needs of persons. Jesus was growing his church when he prayed for the unity of his followers. He was growing his church when he endured the cross. He was growing his church when he appeared to certain persons after his resurrection. Jesus was growing his church when he gave it the Great Commission. He has been growing his church ever since those exciting events at Pentecost. And he is growing his church right up to this very hour!

4. Growth Is Achieved Through a Partnership Effort

Although church growth is always produced by God it is also achieved in partnership with Christians. There is a unique collaboration between the work of God and the activity of man. This collaboration is a divine/human enterprise. It is the will of

God at work in the people of God. It is the initiative of God using his redeemed people in a search for responsive individuals. This is to say that God deems it wise to use human instrumentality in bringing other persons to himself. In this divine/human partnership, God provides all of the resources and man provides the effort. It seems to be a part of God's electing grace to involve men in his redemptive plan. He does this by using human instrumentality in the preparation and consummation of the spiritual harvest.

God has committed to his churches the mission of his Son. And the churches are responsible for the continuation of Christ's mission on earth. They are accountable to him for the conduct of that mission. This partnership between God and man magnifies the church as a distinctive and an unparalleled enterprise. A church is at one and the same time a *divine organism* and a *human organization*. It is *divine in its origin*, but *human in its being*. It is *divine in its ownership* but *human in its membership*. A church is *divine in its fellowship* but *human in its relationships*. It is *divine in its mission*, but *human in its performance*. It is *divine in its growth*, but *human in its outreach*.

Sometimes an objection is raised about the concern for church growth on the grounds that it is too humanistic. But is it? Is church growth of man or is it of God? Or, is church growth a matter of partnership between God and man? Paul seemed to think that it is a partnership matter. When he wrote to the church at Corinth, he reminded the members that he had planted, Apollos had watered, but God had given the increase. Furthermore, he discounted both the planting and watering by indicating that these activities would be rewarded according to effort. It was God who made the difference. The harvest is always in the hands of God, but the work rests in the hands of persons whom God chooses to use. Such an arrangement is a divine/human relationship which redounds to the glory of God. It is the partnership which Paul described as "labourers together with God" (1 Cor. 3:9).

5. Growth Is Enhanced by God's Gifts

In any serious consideration of the growth of the New Testament churches, it would be impossible to ignore the several passages of Scripture which deal with the charismata, the spiritual gifts. In the "gift list" passages (1 Cor. 12:8-10,28; Rom. 12:6-8; Eph. 4:11-12; and 1 Pet. 4:11), there seems to be two levels of spiritual gifts. One level is described as the "greater gifts" which are listed in the Ephesians passage. In the 1 Corinthians 12 passage, the "lesser gifts" are listed. Likely the "greater gifts" were temporary gifts to help the churches while there were no scriptural directions. This concept would indicate that the "lesser gifts," which were functional in nature, were specifically related to the assimilation phase of church growth following the first great wave of growth. There is little doubt that the primary, or greater gifts were related to the period of rapid geographical expansion. The secondary, or lesser, gifts, appear to be more appropriate to the more settled state of the churches. This interpretation seems credible because of the different type of leadership needed in a more stable church situation.

Because the New Testament books were not written for some thirty to sixty years after Pentecost, there were no inspired Scriptures beyond the Old Testament. Neither were there any formal doctrines or systems of theology. Nevertheless, many churches were founded and firmly established in the faith. The conclusion must be drawn that the *charismata*, the special gifts of God, not only enhanced the growth of these early churches but actually made that growth possible. These "greater gifts" were *persons* who had unusual abilities. And these *person gifts* were shared by the various churches. All of the Christians did not have these special gifts. Paul said: "And he gave some, . . . " (Eph. 4:11). Note that *not all* were to be specially gifted. In listing the special persons, Paul noted that some were apostles, the twelve who assisted Jesus; some were prophets, to deepen the understanding of the churches; some were evangelists, to preach the gospel; some were pastors, to shepherd the church; and some were teachers, to guide the growth of the members. These persons were God-gifted and God-given to the churches. They were in a sense officeholders. The temporary nature of most of these offices and gifts probably grew out of the changing circumstances. This period of time was a *transition from Christian Judaism to Gentile Christianity*. The unusual gifts of special persons were needed to equip the new Gentile Christians to fulfill the mission of Christ through these new churches, and at the same time to enable the church to develop according to its unique nature. Although these "offices" seem to have ceased with the death of that generation of special leaders, the functions still remain.

Following this transition period, spiritual gifts seem to become less important. In fact, the biblical references to gifts appear to diminish as the churches matured. There also is an apparent shift from gifts as *persons* to gifts as *functions*. All of the members of the church were admonished to function in a coordinate relationship to each other, as members of a body. The functions performed appeared to be abilities which were innate, as well as new endowments which emerged with the new birth. There is little reason to doubt that the second birth could produce special capacities just as the first birth brings latent talent.

Although the discovery and identification of special gifts is a matter of great personal interest, it is difficult to make a case for them as an unfailing endowment for every Christian. The Scriptures do not require special *gifts* for leadership or service. However, special *qualifications* are required. The fact that the Holy Spirit lives within every regenerated person means that each Christian is *supernaturally endowed* with the potential to become everything God desires him to be. Therefore, it becomes the responsibility of the church to equip its members "unto all good works" (2 Tim. 3:17*b*).

6. Growth Is Related to the Spiritual State of a Church

There is an extraordinary relationship between the growth of a church and the spiritual condition of that church. And, because the process of church growth and the spirituality of a church are such complex matters, it is very difficult to determine whether the relationship is a cause-and-effect connection or simply a correlational matter. Nevertheless, there is abundant evidence that growth rarely occurs when the spiritual climate of a church is lukewarm or cold. There is also considerable confirmation that growth occurs when the spiritual fires are burning brightly. These two interrelated facts seem to indicate that there may be a third factor involved in growth. If so, it would be a force which creates spirituality and causes church growth. Since the Holy Spirit is the source of spirituality and because church growth is essentially a spiritual matter, it is evident that the Holy Spirit is the causative agent in both the spiritual vigor of a church and the growth of a church.

The fact that several types of churches, denominations, and non-Christian religions are enjoying rapid growth raises a serious question: Can adherents to false teaching, and false religions increase readily when sound and orthodox churches fail to grow? The reluctant answer is yes. How can this incongruous situation be? The answer is that many people are easily deceived. Others can be persuaded, even pressured, into accepting error and making unwise commitments. Moreover, charismatic personality, mass manipulation, rhetorical brilliance, logic, and even demagoguery are powerful forces in securing a following. Therefore, church growth *by itself* is not always a valid proof of either a godly leader or a genuine congregation of the Lord. On the other hand, there are numerous churches which seem to have the aura of spirituality, yet they do not grow. Regardless of these seeming inconsistencies, church growth and church spirituality coincide in a very singular fashion. They coalesce into a significant force which causes a church both to grow numerically and to flourish spiritually.

These observations seem to mean two things: (1) When a church grows, it ought to be conscious of the Holy Spirit's presence and power in its midst. However, a growing church should in no way reflect a proud attitude about its success. Furthermore, if a church is not growing, it should not seek to become more spiritual just so it will grow. That would be an improper motivation. (2) When a church is not growing, it ought to become deeply concerned about its responsibility for bringing persons to Christ. It should also rejoice when it grows as a consequence of its outreach and witnessing. Similarly, if a church is not growing, it would be folly to seek to grow simply because it wants to become a spiritual giant in the ecclesiastical world. This, too, would be an improper motivation.

Because of the close connection between numerical growth and the spiritual state of a church, every church should be concerned about its spiritual development. Even more importantly, a church should strive to be a spiritual church simply because it *is* a church. Likewise, because of the vital relationship between spiritual power and church growth, a church cannot tolerate a nongrowth stagnation. Both of these situations belittle the church, betray Christ's Commission, and thwart the work of the Holy Spirit.

Because the spiritual state of a church is so closely related to its ability to grow, it would be helpful if the characteristics of a spiritual church were properly understood. These suggestions may be useful:

(1) A spiritual church recognizes Jesus Christ as its head and accepts his lordship over the church and its individual members.

(2) A spiritual church understands that the church is God's instrument for bringing persons to himself.

(3) A spiritual church accepts every member as a vital part of the body of Christ and loves each as a brother or sister in Christ.

(4) A spiritual church develops its members into a smoothly functioning team and uses them according to their gifts and talents.

(5) A spiritual church lives in the spirit of *koinonia* (bond of fellowship) to such a degree that petty selfishness and worldliness are minimal.

(6) A spiritual church puts great emphasis on Bible study, prayer, and outreach.

(7) A spiritual church ministers in the name of Christ to the needs of its members and prospective members.

(8) A spiritual church, both as individual Christians and as a corporate body, seeks to reproduce itself.

(9) A spiritual church sets its "affections on things above, not on things on the earth" (Col. 3:2).

7. Growth Is Essential to the Continuity of a Church

It is a well-known and self-evident axiom that a church is just one generation away from extinction. This truth is based on the spiritual facts of life. Just as life cannot survive in any species apart from the reproductive process, so a church as a living organism cannot survive apart from the process of making disciples. In this sense, proclamation is paramount to propagation. Regardless of any set of circumstances the making of disciples is the very lifeblood of a church. Anytime a church fails at this task, for whatever reasons, it is committing spiritual suicide.

By virture of its specific assignment in the Great Commission a church exists in the world for one specific purpose—to serve the redemptive mission of Christ. This redemptive occupation makes a church the reincarnation of Christ in a very practical sense. However, if a church fails to be redemptive, it forfeits its birthright and ceases to be an authentic body of Christ. The result is that the church becomes weak and ineffective. It ceases to grow and the seeds of decay begin to sprout. Death is inevitable.

There are other reasons why churches sometimes die. Such things as severe sociological change, single-issue doctrinal disagreements, selective outreach practices, controlled evangelism patterns, internal power struggles, and human malevolence can singly, or in combination cause a church to die. Probably the *lack of a will to live is the most prevalent cause of church death.*

Although some churches may serve their day and pass off the scene, the church as the body of Christ will not die. Such a death is impossible for Jesus said: "The gates of hell [death] shall not prevail against it" (Matt. 16:18).

The church is here to stay—until the Lord comes to claim it as his own. Meanwhile, churches *must* grow. And while growth is not the sole task of a church, it is the one accomplishment without which all others eventually come to naught.

3

The Divine Process in Church Growth

Process is important in any enterprise. For example, the architect has a blueprint—a process design. The dressmaker has a pattern—a process design. The coach has a game plan—a process design. The traveler has a road map—a process design. A church has the Great Commission, and that, too, is a process design, a design for church growth.

By definition, a process design is a graphic representation of the steps, operations, or activities required in reaching an objective. The process in church growth, in and of itself, is not sacred or divine. Actually its significance grows out of the end result which it produces—church growth.

In the church growth context, the phrase "make disciples" in Matthew's account of the Great Commission (28:19-20, RSV) includes the essential requirements for church growth and implies the process by which disciples are to be made.

Because of the "proof text" approach to teaching and preaching, the Great Commission has often been twisted, distorted, and misapplied so profusely that to most people it either means everything or nothing. Nevertheless, the Great Commission is the Magna Charta of the church and has high value in determining the life and work of a church. However, because it has been used to "prove" so many superimposed concepts, it deserves a more careful exegesis.

The fact that the passage in Matthew contains only one

imperative, "make disciples," is well known and widely accepted. It is also fairly well accepted that the English words *going, baptizing,* and *teaching* are only verb forms or participles. An overemphasis on these facts which are only a *part* of the whole has resulted in a general feeling that *going, baptizing,* and *teaching* are weak, if not insignificant, concepts when compared to the imperative phrase "make disciples." If the Greek word for "go ye" (*poreuomai*) were only a simple participle, it would be translated *when you go, as you are going,* or *while you are going.* However, this word along with the Greek words for *baptizing* and *teaching* are *coordinate* participles. This grammatical construction means two things: (1) the words *going, baptizing,* and *teaching* receive their strength from the imperative "make disciples"; (2) because of this unique relationship to the imperative, these words share the same strength as the imperative. Therefore, these participles should also be translated in the imperative mood. Barclay in his *New Translation of the New Testament* makes this grammatical distinctive clear when he translates the passage, "You *must* therefore go and make the people of all nations my disciples. You *must* baptize them in the name of the Father and of the Son and of the Holy Spirit, and you *must* teach them to obey all the commands I have given you" (Matt. 28:19-20, author's italics).

Most church growth specialists tend to separate the concepts of going, baptizing, and teaching from their imperative "make disciples." From their perspective, *going, baptizing,* and *teaching* are mere incidentals, and *conversion* becomes the goal with the very obvious result that there are many converts but few disciples. Such a view is unwarranted. The Greek words for going, baptizing, and teaching are concomitant aspects of making disciples; that is, they must accompany each other—*they must all go together.* Therefore, going, baptizing, and teaching are *ways of making disciples, and they are inherently required by the process of discipling.* Furthermore, the going, baptizing, and teaching concepts are *inclusive examples* and *not exclusive parts* of the discipling process. Going, baptizing, and teaching are essential to making disciples, but there are other approaches as well. Some of these approaches are inherent in the discipling process. Others are found in related passages of Scripture.

Because the concept of making disciples is so frequently viewed primarily as a matter of eliciting "decisions for Christ," producing "professions of faith," "winning souls," or simply as "evangelism," it seems that there is a wide-spread conceptual flaw. This flaw is extremely serious because it appears to equate making disciples with *midwifing the second birth*. Such a concept all but ignores the *human* responsibility for going, the *church* responsibility for baptizing, and the *personal* responsibility for growing. It reduces making disciples to a terminus rather than a continuum.

Perhaps a definition of the phrase "make disciples" would be helpful. To make a disciple is to bring a lost person into (1) a saving relationship with Christ, (2) a maturing relationship with a church, and (3) a witnessing relationship with the world. These three aspects of making disciples are not sequential or chronological. They are not stages through which a convert passes to arrive eventually as a "lettered" Christian. However, there are distinctive time elements involved. First, the saving relationship is an instantaneous happening which is valid through all eternity. It can never be experienced again by the same person. Second, the maturing relationship is lifelong and has observable stages of progress. Third, the witnessing relationship can and should begin immediately following conversion and is to last throughout life.

These vital relationships are developmental in process and spiritual in nature; they flourish when there is adequate attention given to preparation, education, and application. These relationships are the *essence* of the discipling process; they are emphatically *not the result of the process*. But the process is the means by which impediments to growing relationships are removed.

The process of making disciples requires a church to conduct specific activities on both a constant and continuous basis. These continuing activities are not simply matters of current interest, special events, or even the basic program; rather they are the *essence* of a church. They are the evidence of a church actually being a church. A definitive look at some of these activities will be helpful.

1. Being Where Unsaved Persons Can Be Found

Although the Great Commission is undoubtedly incumbent on every church as a corporate body of Christ, the Commission in its specific context was probably given to all of the disciples, with the apostles as a special target group.

The key word in the Commission is *go*. In the New Testament the word is always used in its participial form—that is, *going*. In absolute constructions a participle may modify a whole sentence. In the Commission the word *go* becomes the *basic action on which all the other activities are dependent*. In addition, the word carries the idea of procedure or method. Therefore, the word *go* means going from place to place. The concept of going from place to place was given much more meaning when Jesus said to his apostles, "Ye shall be witnesses unto me both in Jerusalem, and in all Judaea, and in Samaria, and unto the uttermost part of the earth" (Acts 1:8*b*). The idea was to disciple Jerusalem and then to proceed from Jerusalem to the entire civilized world.

The response of the apostles was remarkable. In the vernacular, they "got going!" In the process they grew churches in Jerusalem, Samaria, Antioch, Joppa, Caesarea, Philippi, Thessalonica, Berea, Athens, Corinth, Ephesus, Colossae, and Rome. Eventually they seemed to have gone as far as India, Persia, Great Britain, and Armenia (which is now partitioned among Iran, Turkey, and Russia). It is thought by some scholars that Bartholomew died in Russia. All the evidence indicates that the apostles understood completely what Jesus meant when he said "go." And they certainly knew what he meant when he said "make disciples."

Probably the greatest problem faced by churches today is the fact that they are not actually going where lost people are to be found. Even though church buildings are generally surrounded by non-Christians, most churches do little more than "be nice" to persons who come to the church building of their own accord. Few churches know the name, address, and spiritual condition of the people in their contiguous community, much less in their larger field of responsibility. Few churches have any systematic approach to *going* into their own world. Some even erect barriers for persons who dare to come on their own initiative.

The appalling truth is that many churches are not only failing to grow; they do not desire to grow, and some even want *not* to grow. These attitudes are completely foreign to the directive which Jesus gave his church. His command was to disciple *all* nations. His literal words were *ta ethna* all peoples. The phrase refers to the total concept of people. It means every kind of person from all kinds of peoples.

To the Jews this was a difficult concept. They were a proud people—children of Abraham. They were a select nation— God's Chosen People. They were a theocracy—a nation under God. But the Commission ignored those magnificent facts; it made everyone equal and everyone equally responsible for all people. They must have reasoned, why couldn't Christ simply restore the kingdom of Israel? Why would he ignore both nationalism and religion and reach out to "all these people" who had no national entity or religious faith? Could Christ *really* mean *every* nation—all of those non-Jews? All of those Gentile dogs? All of those despised Samaritans? All of those Roman pagans? All of those unbelieving infidels?

Amazingly enough the Jewish Christians responded affirmatively. As a church they saw themselves as a new people *on mission for Christ* in the world, and themselves as members who were *missionaries to the world*. Every member was a minister who discharged his responsibility both to the church body and to his own special world of non-Christians. Every member was willing and eager to become equipped "for every good work." They *wanted* to participate in the invasion of the unbelieving world and bear witness to the Light that had come into darkness.

Any contemporary church which wants to make disciples must find a way to *be where unsaved people are.* By and large the unsaved people are not in the church buildings. "They do not *come* (to church), they must be *brought*; they will not *seek*, they must be *sought*." It is becoming increasingly clear that if non-Christians are to be won *by the church*, they must be won *away from the church building.* At least in most instances the visitation and cultivation activities must be initiated in some other place.

Interestingly enough, there is little if any biblical evidence that direct evangelism was the purpose of New Testament church gatherings. Evangelism was certainly not an "in-house" program. As a matter of fact, in New Testament times there were no church buildings. The first church building was erected during the reign of Alexander Severus who reigned AD 222-235. If the early churches were to make disciples, they had no choice: *they had to go where the people were.* They could not depend on a sensational sanctuary, a prestigious pastor, a scintillating staff, a bountiful budget, a musical montage, a self-serving program, or a personality parade. All they could do was to *pray* for power, *knock* on doors, *witness* to their faith, *share* the gospel, *plead* for repentance, and *baptize* the new converts!

Churches as bodies and Christians as individual ministers of Christ must rediscover and practice their priority responsibility. That priority is proclamation, rightly understood. Pulpit preaching is involved, but proclamation is essentially *teaching, witnessing, and declaring the good news of the gospel.* And not at the church building only, but everywhere! If a church is to make disciples, that responsibility must come back to the individual members; and the members must discharge that responsibility wherever they *are* and wherever they can *go*. When they do, churches will grow because disciples will be made.

2. Sharing the Gospel with Persons Who Will Listen

Contemporary Christianity is largely characterized by a spirit of shallow activism. The light rejoinder "do something even if it is wrong" depicts the whirlwind approach to everything *except* sharing the good news of Jesus Christ. How tragic!

Although the Bible teaches direct access to God, it also makes the Christian an agent of reconciliation. This assignment places the Christian in a unique position between the desperate need of man and God's marvelous provision for that need. This relational aspect of evangelism is essential because in the vast majority of cases unsaved persons can be brought to God only as the good news is shared on a one-to-one basis. Generally this type of sharing is best done in the everyday routines of life. By using all of the natural methods of communication, Christians can and should literally give themselves away in a sincere, sensible, and significant sharing of the gospel. This type of sharing should be viewed as the normal and natural way to "bring men to God through Jesus Christ." It was so considered in New Testament times. It was so demonstrated by the Bible characters which most Christians honor and admire. It is written of those early believers that "all day in the Temple and from house to house they never stopped teaching and telling the good news that Jesus was the Messiah" (Acts 5:42, Barclay).

Just as sharing some item of good news with friends is a normal and enjoyable activity, so should sharing with unsaved persons the *good news about Christ* be a natural and enjoyable act for Christians. Sharing can and should be an unfeigned manner of communication. It need not, and probably should not, be a professional approach to evangelism. It ought not be a pressured or manipulative broadside designed to coerce persons into making an unwilling profession.

The fact that a Christian himself has experienced redemption from sin, plus the knowledge that witnessing is required of all believers, is all that is required to share the gospel. However, it is wise to become knowledgeable in the message of the gospel, approaches to witnessing, and the essentials of follow-up activities.

The purpose of this discussion is not to present ways of witnessing. Rather it is designed to (1) emphasize the fact that making *converts* is the job of every Christian, and (2) stress the point that making *disciples* is the job of every church. These two perspectives make it clear that the evangelistic thrust of the gospel is (1) *generated* by the churches in their corporate discipling *inside* the building, and (2) *expended* by the individual members as they witness *outside* the building. These truths mean that as an agency of God's kingdom, a church must both make disciples and mobilize its members for making disciples. It also means that as church members and as individual disciples, Christians must share the gospel with their own personal world. Only in this way can a church fulfill its mission. And only in this way can a member give valid proof of his personal discipleship.

These concepts, which are thoroughly biblical in nature, should not be interpreted to mean that efforts to evangelize at the church building should be discontinued. That assumption would be in error, because there are biblical examples of both *going* and *coming*. These aforementioned concepts actually support *bidirectional* evangelism. Church growth has always been characterized by an outward moving power which is generated by its inward moving strength. These two forces are not in any way opposite forces. Rather, these two forces sustain each other. Both are required for obedience to the Great Commission, and both are essential to keeping alive the creative tension between a lost world and the people of God. Nevertheless, an alarming truth remains: Christians are broadly negligent in their responsibility to share the gospel. They are either unwilling to try, or they lack the ability to share effectively. And widespread failure is producing a negative impact on a positive sharing of the gospel.

3. Helping Responsive Persons Come to Christ

Next to knowing how to witness appropriately to one's own faith in Christ, nothing is more important to the Christian than the ability to help an unsaved person make a decisive commitment to Christ. Making such a commitment is generally a difficult matter because it goes against the nature of an unsaved person. The life patterns, the pleasures of sin, the strength of habit, the tendency toward inertia, and the power of Satan all combine to create a resistance to the urge to yield to Christ. Furthermore, conquering the hold of sin, resisting the power of unbelief, and overcoming the fear of taking a public stand for Christ, requires a high degree of courage and determination. Often, the strong quiver with fear, while the timid shrink with dread, when they contemplate making an open profession of faith in Christ. At the very time a decision is imminent, Satan uses his strongest deterrent by suggesting a delay. Just as Felix opted for "a [more] convenient season" (Acts 24:25) when he was confronted with the gospel by the apostle Paul, Satan seems to always make postponement seem so very wise.

It is at the point of decision that Christians can be most helpful. When the decisive moment arrives, both the courage and determination of the unsaved person may readily be reinforced with a little help from an interested Christian. The hesitant person can be encouraged by a friendly handclasp, a word of reinforcement, a sentence or two of prayer, and a gentle reminder that millions of other persons have already made this decision. Because of the eternal consequences that are involved, it is always in order to be considerately supportive, encouraging, and alert to the opportunity to show a sense of urgency.

In helping persons respond to Christ as Savior, it is well to remember that Jesus did not beg or overpersuade anyone to accept him. In fact, there is no biblical record of any Christian who witnessed by any type of coercive action. It is true that Jesus appealed to the best self-interest of the rich young ruler but he let him go when he turned away sadly. When Paul made his strong appeal to King Agrippa (Acts 26), he did not persist, pester, or pressure the king to make a commitment.

Helping persons respond to Christ does not depend on human importunity, persistence, or undue persuasion. It is much more appropriate to be a loving support system through which the Holy Spirit may do his own work of convicting and converting.

4. Bringing Believers into Church Fellowship

Inherent in the response to Christ is the need for fellowship with other Christians and a positive relationship with a local body of Christ. Therefore, a new convert needs to take three specific actions: (1) make a public profession of faith; (2) accept baptism into the church membership; and (3) develop a growing sense of commitment to Christ and the Christian faith.

It would seem to be most obvious that baptism and church membership have nothing to do with one's salvation. It would also seem obvious that salvation has everything to do with baptism and church membership, because both of these are post-salvation experiences. These observations not only point up the relationship between salvation and church membership, they also magnify the significance of each one. Jesus himself submitted to baptism, and he included it in his Commission to the church. At first glance, church membership seems to be simply the end result of baptism. However, membership is the basis of acceptance into the body of Christ in its local expression. Because a church is a singular expression of a unique relationship between God and man, and because a church functions as a body of Christ, church membership constitutes entitlement to the functions of the family of God.

New Christians will not grow into *disciples* outside of the context of a church. A relational fellowship to other Christians is essential to the strength of a new Christian. The experiences within a church are critical to the maturation of the new Christian. The learning within the church is basic to the service rendered by the new Christian. When Jesus said, "teaching them to observe all things," he commanded his church to service the growth needs of new Christians. And by tacit inference he expects persons who believe in him to accept the efforts of the church to help them progress through the various stages of discipleship.

These concepts speak loudly to both a church and a new Christian. To the church the message is integrate, assimilate, educate, indoctrinate, and motivate all new converts. To the new Christian, the message is affiliate, participate, investigate, incorporate, and animate!

5. Involving New Members in Vital Relationships

Just as baptism is the door to church membership, so is membership the entrance into church fellowship. But these are only entry-level attainments. The whole field of relationships lies ahead. The fellowship *of a church* and the fellowship *within a church* are two dimensions of a unique relationship. This relationship has a distinct social character, but it is far more than just another social relationship. Church fellowship is also highly dynamic, but it is far more than just another source of energy and vitality. Church fellowship is extremely relational in its nature. This fellowship is *based* on the Christian's relation to God through Jesus Christ, and it is *realized* through the Christian's relationship to other believers. Christian fellowship involves both a vertical relationship with God and a horizontal relationship with other Christians. Both of these relationships are *positional*. They are the result of being "in Christ." These two positions are also *relational*. They are the outgrowth of essential experiences with God and vital experiences with fellow Christians. Furthermore, these relationships and experiences are interrelated, if not inseparable. They grow out of, and are developed by, the spiritual dynamics which are generated by Bible study, prayer, witnessing, and all the other interpersonal experiences involved in serving Christ as fellow members of his body.

These extraordinary relationships and experiences are described by the Greek word *koinonia*. This word has rich, multifaceted meanings. It means such things as having or holding something in common, giving and taking in the process of sharing, having a part in, participating jointly, communicating, associating together, and have specific types of fellowship. *Koinonia* implies a mutuality of participation and a reciprocity of result. For example, when Christians visit prospects together (an action) they experience *koinonia* in the process (a result). There is, therefore, a cause-and-effect dimension to Christian relationships. Both aspects grow out of the fact that Christ is the common bond between Christians. And the relationship involved in being fellow disciples is the dynamic which produces fellowship.

But a word of caution is in order. When fellowship becomes the *goal* of a church rather than the *spirit* of a church, there can be danger ahead. A church may become so intent on developing its fellowship that it overlooks the purpose of fellowship. The ultimate purpose is to strengthen and motivate the members to reach out, to share the *koinonia* with the unreached. If reaching out begins to die out, the *koinonia* has degenerated into mere social fellowship. And the church has become, or is becoming, ingrown, stale, and superficial. Staying in close touch with the lost world is the only way to keep a church alive and vital. And the activities required to keep the church "in touch" are the very same activities which Christians must participate in if they are to experience *koinonia*.

6. Teaching Church Members the Word of Truth

Just as *making disciples* is the essence of the Great Commission, so is *teaching* the essence of making disciples. This truth probably accounts for the fact that the New Testament is filled with admonitions to teach and illustrations of the significance of teaching.

The word *disciple* is in itself a commentary on the importance of teaching. A disciple is a *learner*, and being a learner implies being taught. In reality, *a Christian becomes a disciple only as he is taught and as he responds by learning*. Thus, teaching and learning are the *process* while discipleship is the *product*.

Early in the Book of Acts it is evident that the first response of new Christians was a desire for a knowledge of the Word of Truth. Acts 2:42 records, "And they continued stedfastly in the apostles' doctrine" (teaching). Apparently Christ's command to teach was reinforced with a divinely implanted desire for learning. This conjoinment seems to undergird the divine and human aspects of the disciple-making process.

Although there are several words for teaching found in the Greek New Testament, *didasko* is by far the most prominent. It means: (1) the act of instruction, teaching; (2) the content to be taught, doctrine; and (3) the persons taught, learners. The word occurs frequently in the Gospels, in Acts, and in the Epistles. Significantly the word *didasko* is used to describe the teaching of lost persons as often as it is used to portray the doctrinal instruction of the saved.

The biblical emphasis in teaching is not concerned with principles, methods, settings, procedures, and techniques. It is concerned with the communication of truth. As a matter of fact, all forms of discourse in the New Testament have a didactic distinctive. In a day when process and groupness have all but become the goal of education, it should be remembered that *content is the cargo of communication*.

In the Jewish society of New Testament times the profession of teaching was well established and highly honored. The scribes (rabbis) preserved and interpreted the law. The synagogues served as an educational setting, and the services were largely educational in nature. Jesus himself, though not a professional teacher, was acknowledged to be "a teacher come from God" by a religious leader of his day. Throughout his earthly ministry he gave his attention primarily to education. He *taught* the multitudes, he *equipped* the disciples, he *trained* the apostles, and he *mentored* Peter, James, and John. He *instructed* Peter individually.

The apostle Paul was a leading advocate of teaching and learning. After his conversion to Christ he eagerly received instruction from Ananias. He spent three learning years in the desert. He became a teaching apostle, a doctrinal preacher, an equipping missionary. Under the inspiration of the Holy Spirit he penned the great doctrines—teachings, truths—of the church.

Teaching and learning—the disciple-making process—is a noble heritage of both the Jewish religion and the Christian faith. But teaching and learning are not ends in themselves. They are the support system for *disciples*.

But what should a disciple know? What should he learn? What should he be taught? Many things, of course. The following list contains the essentials:

(1) A disciple needs to *understand* his relationship to Christ.

(2) A disciple needs to *know* what is required of disciples.

(3) A disciple needs to be *taught* and to become a student of the Bible.

(4) A disciple needs to *learn* how to live the truths the Bible teaches.

(5) A disciple needs to *comprehend* his responsibility for sharing Christ and be able to share.

(6) A disciple needs to *prepare* to be a lifelong minister of Jesus Christ.

(7) A disciple needs to *develop* a life-style that is positively Christian.

7. Equipping Members for the Work of Ministry

One of the most widely misunderstood concepts of Christian service is the ministry function (*diakonia*) of the church members. Insofar as the New Testament churches were concerned, the terms "Christian," "disciple," and "minister" were synonyms. Both in theological meaning and in practical application there were no real differences. They were all "partners working together for God" (1 Cor. 3:9, TEV). *All* members of the church were considered to be ministers (*diakonos*) of Jesus Christ. To be sure, there were pastors (*poimen*), even a multiplicity of pastors, in many churches. Also, there were many teachers (*didaskalos*). All of these special ministers served as equippers of the saints. They were never considered to be "clergy."

The ministering roles and the essential abilities were considered to be the result of "grace gifts" (charismata) provided by the Holy Spirit. These gifts were to be used to edify, build up, and strengthen the church for its task of making disciples. Paul, the biblical authority on church matters, expressed it this way: "There are distinctive gifts of grace, but the same Spirit, and there are distinctive ministries, yet the same Lord. There are also varieties of things accomplished, but the same God does all the energizing in them all" (1 Cor. 12:4-6, Berkeley). In this passage Paul emphasized (1) the variety of ministries; (2) the source of the gifts; and (3) the significance of the ministers.

Just as the early disciples and the twelve apostles needed to be trained and equipped, so do all contemporary believers. This need grows out of the fact that the Christian mission has not changed, and the assignment to the churches remains constant. All believers are *required* to become disciples. In fact, the original meanings of these words are essentially synonymous. Therefore, all Christians need to be *equipped*, to be *prepared* for the work of ministry.

Because equipping is a part of the process of making disciples, and because the Commission *requires* churches to make disciples, it follows that a church is derelict in its obedience to Christ when it fails to equip its members. It is no disparagement of evangelism to note that churches generally have been long on evangelism and short on discipling. This unfortunate imbalance has created an unscriptural dichotomy between conversion and discipleship. The result is that making *converts* has been substituted for making *disciples*. In the process, evangelism has become a *profession* of the clergy and a few "super" saints, rather than the *occupation* of all Christians. Meanwhile multitudes of persons have made decisions, even professions of faith, without experiencing any vital commitment to Christ. These persons have become converts perhaps, but certainly not *disciples*. Many have not even become church members. This approach to evangelism is comparable to equating parenting with childbearing. Both of these concepts are incredulously incongruous.

It is time for churches to realize that their objective is to *make disciples*. It is also time to eliminate the unwarranted and competitive differences between evangelism and education. Both of these matters are equally significant because they are simply parts of a much larger whole—making disciples!

8. Involving New Disciples in the Work of the Church

As a body of believers a church is the context for making disciples. Only in a church can the essential ingredients be provided: nurture, fellowship, caring relationships, encouragement, instruction in discipleship, spiritual exercise, and proper motivation. Only in a church can the gifts, talents, and skills required for "the perfecting of the saints" (Eph. 4:12) be found. Only in a church can valid models of discipleship (servanthood) be found.

Unfortunately many new Christians fail to grow into useful disciples. Sometimes this failure grows out of refusal to participate in discipleship training. Many times the failure to grow can be traced to the church's failure to provide the essentials of growth. More often there is the lack of any real effort to involve new members in the edification process of the church.

There are three serious problems which churches need to face in the matter of involving members in the work: (1) the overloading of the faithful few; (2) the use of willing but unqualified persons; (3) the failure to develop and use new people. Interestingly, the solving of the third problem solves the other two. The way to unload the overloaded and to qualify the unqualified is to develop and use more people.

The same reasoning applies to making disciples. In his letter to Timothy, Paul said: "The things you have learned from me before many witnesses you must commit to trustworthy men who will be competent to teach others too" (2 Tim. 2:2, Williams).

In essence Paul gave a formula for making effective disciples: (1) learn, (2) commit, and (3) teach. In other words, (1) give instruction, (2) seek a commitment, and (3) use appropriately.

Undoubtedly the New Testament teaches that God gives gifts (both persons *and* abilities) to his *churches*. Some eighteen or twenty of these giftings are listed as examples of God's provision for his work in the churches. As far as is feasible, churches need to identify their own divine allotment of gifts and *find a place* for these persons to serve. This concept is quite different from the typical concern about finding someone to fill some vacancy.

Involving new members in the work of the church is a definite and distinctive aspect of making disciples. It is slow and difficult work. Nevertheless, God's gifts include persons who are effective in this important work.

Becoming a Christian is indeed a *new birth*. More than that, it is the door to *new life*. It is a door which opens a whole new world of learning, growth, and development as a *disciple* of Jesus Christ.

Helping another person come to a saving knowledge of Christ is a wonderful experience. But helping that person move into spiritual maturity and usefulness as a servant of Christ is equally rewarding and perhaps more demanding. This long and tedious effort may be what causes the eventual result to seem so fulfilling.

"Go therefore and *make disciples*" (Matt. 28:19, RSV, author's italics).

4

The Basic Strategy in Church Growth

Success in any venture is largely a matter of having and using a well-defined strategy. This basic principle is especially applicable to the growth of a church. Therefore, any significant success in making disciples of Jesus Christ, and in relating them positively to a local church, waits on the use of an authentic growth strategy. This concept of strategy takes into account the spiritual dynamics involved in church growth.

Consider the meaning of the word *strategy*. In its exact sense, the word is a Greek derivative which refers to a military generalship. In that context a strategy is simply the way in which human and material resources are used to support a military objective. However, in its larger meaning, the word *strategy* refers to any basic plan for conducting any type of venture. From that perspective, a strategy of church growth would be a plan of action that is effective in making disciples and in bringing about a desirable quantity and quality of church growth.

At first thought the very suggestion of using a strategy to grow a church may seem crass, if not wholly out of harmony with the nature of any religious enterprise. In fact, even the idea of church *strategetics* might appear to some to be foreign to the purpose and work of the Spirit of God. But is that conclusion really valid? Is the human penchant for working according to a plan alien to working within the will of God? Is there any possibility that God would bless a church-growth strategy? More pertinently, is there some biblical evidence that God himself has already established a strategy for building a church? In the light of these queries another question begins to emerge: Is there a biblical strategy for church growth? The anticipated answer is almost as apparent: Yes, there is a very clear biblical strategy for growing a church. Furthermore, that strategy has been tested, validated, and authenticated both in New Testament times and in contemporary settings. The strategy is as simple as it is authentic. In its essence the church growth strategy is *making adults the primary target in evangelism.*

A strategy of adult evangelism is not some new fad of church growth experts. It is not a promotional scheme with an age-group twist. It is not an effort to magnify adults. And it is certainly not an attempt to discredit other age groups. On a more positive note, the strategy of adult evangelism is un-mistakably biblical. *There is no other approach to evangelism found in the New Testament.*

If a strategy of growth based on adults as the target group of evangelism seems forced or superimposed, it would be well to remember that there are numerous strategies found in the Bible. For example, there was the *strategy of choice* when God selected Abram to become the father of the Hebrew nation. There was the *strategy of gender* when God placed on men the major responsibility for the religious leadership of the family. There was the *strategy of race* when God selected the Jewish people to become his chosen nation. There was the *strategy of locale* when God gave the Promised Land to his Chosen People. There was the *strategy of influence* when God made adults responsible for the religious education of their children. There was the *strategy of accountability* when God made the church responsible for evangelizing the world. Therefore, the *strategy of adult evangelism* is quite in harmony with God's way of doing things.

It is quite possible that the New Testament churches made an effort to evangelize persons of all ages; if they did, these efforts are not recorded in the Bible. On the other hand, the Bible is full of references to the fact that those early believers gave priority to adult evangelism. They taught adults, they visited adults, they preached to adults, they witnessed to adults, they healed adults, they ministered to adults, they prayed for adults, and in many cases they gave their lives in a Christian testimony before adults. There is no inductive reasoning and no deductive logic that can avoid the conclusion that there was an adult strategy involved in the methodology of the New Testament churches. An adult-focused evangelism must not be considered as a strategy to glorify adults. It is a strategy that glorifies God. It is a tribute to his great wisdom. This approach to evangelism does point up the influential role of adults in all aspects of life. It emphasizes the wisdom of winning adults as the way to win all persons. It is important to realize that bringing adults to Christ is the key to bringing children, youth, families, towns, and entire countries to God.

The adult strategy does not imply a value difference between adults and other age groups. A strategy is simply a way to get things done. It is not a matter of discrimination. It does not indicate a divine bias or prejudice. It *is* the divine logistic for reaching the world for Christ. Furthermore, *it is the only plan or pattern of evangelism found in the Bible.*

1. The Strategy Grows Out of a Larger Plan of God

The strategy of an adult-focused evangelism is a highly important principle in church growth. It is probably the most crucial of all principles. However, it is a part of an even larger religious methodology involving adults. God's plan for bringing the world to himself involves working through adults to accomplish his purpose in the world. There is no direct statement in the Bible which says that God's plan for achieving his purpose is an adult-oriented plan. However, from Genesis to Revelation, God is seen at work with adults. The plan is so clearly established that it can readily be stated as a theology of God's use of man. Such a theology would include at least the following concepts.

The adult strategy is divine, not human. Man did not in any way contrive to place himself in God's spotlight. It was God himself who took the initiative in bringing man into focus. It was God who originated the concept of man and who conceived the plan for creating him. By his own volition God took the initiative in creating man from the dust of the earth. It was God's own deliberate act by which he shared his divine likeness with a created being and gave him the privilege of self-control. It was God who gave man the power of autonomy. It was God who gave man the capacity for growth and development. It was God who gave man the full responsibility over creation. And it was God who endowed man with the capacity for everlasting existence.

God, who through his natural laws of life, normally begins all created life with the young of the species, brought man into existence in the mature adult stage of life. In this spectacular act God made possible a direct fellowship and communion between himself and his creative masterpiece. Even after man's fall from his state of innocence into the degradation of sin, God made loving provision for man's rebellion by promising to provide a Redeemer. (See Gen. 3:15.) God's continuing concern for his sinful creature is the central theme of the entire Bible. Thus the drama of redemption is the continuing story of God's compassion for the adult generation of his erring earthlings.

In reviewing these theological truths about man's origin and the subsequent degradation of his high potential, it is important to realize that God always concentrates his attention on the adult generation. In preparing adults for their unique role in his creation God gave them some special privileges and singular opportunities. Along with these magnificent endowments God also assigned adults some distinctive responsibilities which adults alone can perform. And he requires of them a level of accountability which only mature persons can even begin to bear.

When adults failed to obey God, he punished them for their disobedience. Over and over through history he sought to bring them back into fellowship with him and to restore them to the center of his purpose for them. It is unmistakably clear that the biblical revelation is a special message to a special segment of the human race as a special effort to restore man to his magnificent birthright. Undoubtedly God works with the adult generation in accomplishing his will in the world. This was, and is, the ultimate reason for his extraordinary attention to adults.

God's plan for using adults also includes the selection and use of special adults to serve his purpose. For example, God's selection of leaders demonstrated his use of the adult strategy. When God called Abram (Abraham), who was without any doubt an adult, to become the father of a new nation, he was preparing a people who would eventually become a blessing to all nations. "Now the Lord had said unto Abram, Get thee out of thy country, and from thy kindred, and from thy father's house, unto a land that I will shew thee: . . . and I will . . . make thy name great; and thou shalt be a blessing: And I will bless them that bless thee, and curse him that curseth thee: and in thee shall all families of the earth be blessed" (Gen. 12:1-3).

God called Moses, another adult, to serve him in a special leadership capacity. It was to Moses that God gave the basic pattern which became the model for reaching and teaching people. "Gather the people together, men, and women, and children, and thy stranger that is within thy gates, that they may hear, and that they may learn, and fear the Lord your God, and observe to do all the words of this law" (Deut. 31:12). This pattern places men and women in the forefront of all efforts to reach and to teach persons. The pattern emphasizes the family relationships in educational activities but it is very definitely adult centered. Although Moses wrote the passage, it was a directive from God—an adult-oriented directive.

God also prepared a special messenger who was an adult to

become the forerunner of the Messiah. John, the apostle, writing about John the baptizer, said: "There was a man sent from God, whose name was John. The same came for a witness, to bear witness of the Light, that all men through him might believe" (John 1:6-7).

There is an abundance of evidence which points up the fact that *the adult strategy is a divine design.* Not the least of this evidence is the Bible itself. In every respect the Bible is an adult book. Its content was revealed to adults. Its message was recorded by adults. Its thought patterns are specifically aimed at adults. Its literary style is directed toward adults. Its terminology is distinctly adult. Its vocabulary communicates primarily to the adult mind. Its truths are presented largely on an adult level, and its meaning can be fully understood by adults alone. Its applications are made to adult life. Its target audience is both directly and indirectly adult.

The great passages of the Bible have an unqualified appeal to adults and a universal application to adults. The Ten Commandments have a pertinent relevance to adults. The holy covenants were made between God and adults. The major precepts of the Bible are addressed to adults. The grand truths of the Bible were spoken to adults. The renowned instructions found in the Bible were first taught to adults. The judgments pronounced in the Bible were placed on adults. The solemn admonitions of the Bible were given for the benefit of adults. Clearly there is a divine design to the adult-focused strategy.

2. The History of Redemption Is Adult-Oriented

Redemption is the indisputable subject of the Bible. This theme is perceived in a variety of ways. For example, it is often described as "the drama of redemption," "God's redemptive plan," "the doctrine of salvation," and "salvation history."

Regardless of the individual viewpoint or the theological structure used, there is a common characteristic in each of the several approaches to the story of redemption: namely, *God's plan of redemption is always projected on an adult level and presented in an adult frame of reference.* To be sure, redemption is rarely, if ever, labeled as an adult plan. Nevertheless, it is always presented in terms of adult concepts, adult thought patterns, and in adult terminology. In addition, redemption always deals with the realities of adult sin, and it portrays the adult need of salvation.

Salvation is not only the unifying theme of the biblical revelation; it is also a message that is in and of itself uniquely adult in its nature. In its own words the Bible was *theopnuestos* (God breathed out) to chosen adults. It was also recorded by adults, shared with adults, copied for adults, and preserved by adults, all because of its immensely significant meaning to adults.

From book to book, from chapter to chapter, from page to page, the Bible throbs with an urgent appeal to adults. It reveals God's loving concern for lost and wayward adults. It pleads with adults to hear the Word of the Lord. It admonishes adults to give heed to the message. It urges adults to seek the Lord, to return to the God their fathers, and to be reconciled to God.

The Bible presents sin as the mortal enemy of adults, and salvation as God's immortal provision for the redemption of adults. Over and over again the Bible records God's gift of salvation being extended to succeeding generations of adults. Although it is perfectly clear that salvation is for all persons who are capable of a faith commitment to Christ, the presentation of the message of salvation is always given in an adult context. Obviously, God's strategy for accomplishing his redemptive work in the world is unique. It is a strategy of providing salvation especially for adults, and it is communicated to adults in astoundingly pertinent forms.

The biblical history of redemption is so clearly adult oriented that it seems to have been taken for granted through the centuries; or else it has been generally overlooked, ignored, or considered to be of little significance. Nevertheless, the adult focus in salvation history is the most obvious purpose of "God's Mighty Acts" on behalf of mankind.

3. Adult Evangelism Was the Focus of Christ's Ministry

The Gospels are basically a record of Christ's ministry on earth. To say that they are a record of his ministry to adults is simply to state a self-evident truth. Actually, there is no viable evidence that Jesus directed any of his evangelistic efforts toward anyone other than adults. He concentrated his ministry on the adults to the point of seeming to exclude all others, especially in his direct personal contacts with people. The exclusive idea should not be pressed because he preached to the multitudes. Presumably children were in the crowd and youth were almost certainly present. Yet even in these crowds he addressed his message to the adult audience. No doubt Jesus loved the children, but his heart burned with compassion for the adult generation. These observations are made to point out the fact that Jesus had to be aware of the divine strategy and that he followed it himself in his own earthly ministry. All the evidence points to the fact that Jesus was essentially a minister to adults in the full meaning of that concept.

In the early part of his ministry, when Jesus walked by the Sea of Galilee, he recruited two adult men. In this act, Simon and his brother Andrew became his first disciples. These two adults became the nucleus of the group which Jesus described as "fishers of men." This term denoted a special ministry of evangelism with a direct adult thrust. Subsequently Jesus enlisted ten other adult men to complete his evangelistic team. Later he organized the seventy into a separate adult task force comprised of thirty-five teams of two men each. It seems to be a matter of high significance that the very first outreach effort was in every respect a thoroughgoing adult-focused evangelistic program. It can only be described as a program of adults, for adults, to adults, by adults. It is a peerless picture of the divine strategy at work as a New Testament precedent and as a New

Testament pattern of evangelism. There can be no doubt about it—Jesus focused his own ministry and that of his disciples on the adult generation. He assiduously followed the Old Testament prototype by dealing primarily with men, but he also set the new example of total adult outreach by including adult women in his ministry. Furthermore, the disciples understood that the adult focus was involved in the Great Commission, for they did not vary from it in any particular in all of their own ministry. Both during and after Christ's time on earth the disciples were caught up in an intensive evangelistic emphasis that not only included adults but seemed to be totally adult in its nature.

4. Adult Evangelism Was Authenticated by the Holy Spirit

The tendency to be overly concerned about the gift of languages on the Day of Pentecost makes it easy to overlook the real phenomenon that occurred that day. The significant event was not the "tongues" but the witness of adults to adults in a way which the Holy Spirit chose to use in an unusual display of affirmation and power. The apostles, and probably the entire membership of the early church, began to mingle with the thousands of foreign-born Jews and proselytes who had come to Jerusalem for the celebration of Pentecost. What they were doing is not stated, but is it not logical to assume that they were doing what they usually did in a crowd? Were they not teaching and preaching Christ? There is no doubt that they were witnessing in a classic way. They were simply practicing the New Testament method of evangelism. In a nutshell, they were employing the adult strategy. The entire scenario was one of sincere believers sharing in an adult-to-adult manner their witness to the saving grace of God in Jesus Christ. They were doing what Jesus had commanded them only a few days earlier—and they were beginning in Jerusalem as instructed.

However, in their eagerness to witness they ran into a very real problem. The crowd in Jerusalem had come from all over the civilized world, and some twelve to fifteen languages were being spoken. Since these languages were unfamiliar to the local Christians, there was a real communication problem. It was the language barrier that the Holy Spirit used to ignite their witness. In an indescribable manifestation of power the Holy Spirit came upon them to affirm their witness and to make it effective. He gave evidence of his presence in an unprecedented fashion. What appeared to be tongues of fire divided and settled on each witness. Along with this affirmation of power these witnesses were suddenly enabled to speak their witness in languages which they did not know but which were the native tongues to persons who listened. In this way everyone heard the gospel in one's own language. A miracle? Certainly! But it was much more a miracle of witnessing than a miracle of manifestation. There was an evangelistic purpose behind the event, and in a very real way it was the Holy Spirit making the adult strategy effective. It was a divine affirmation of both the gospel itself and the method of those who were giving their witness to Christ. When the curiosity about the language phenomenon is laid aside, the entire event is easily recognized as another aspect of the adult strategy. God was indicating his concern for the adult generation. He was making it possible for interested persons to understand the gospel. Furthermore, God was honoring the faithfulness of his people in making an effective adult-to-adult effort to share the gospel. Although the gospel is for everyone, there can be no doubt about the focus group. *Taking the good news to unsaved adults is the very heart of God's strategy for winning the world to himself.* Any evangelistic approach that ignores this principle or belittles its significance, falls far short of the biblical norm and the unfailing practice of the New Testament churches.

5. Adult Evangelism Is the Key to Family Evangelism

Because of the nature of adulthood and its impact on the younger generations, the adult strategy has had a significant influence in all religious matters. In outreach and evangelism, the adult strategy has proven to be extremely effective. In evangelizing adults, parents are won to Christ and, in the process, entire families come under the influence of the gospel.

Because of this extraordinary fact, adult evangelism takes on a whole new dimension. In effect, winning adults becomes the way to reach whole family units. Thus *adult* evangelism often becomes *family* evangelism. Such an overflow effect is frequently found in the New Testament. For example, when Jesus came to Jericho and found Zacchaeus open to the gospel, he went to visit with him in his home. As a result Zacchaeus responded, as did his entire household. This experience prompted Jesus to say, "For the Son of man is come to seek and to save that which was lost" (Luke 19:10).

Jesus told the pleading nobleman to return to his home because his son who had been grievously ill had been saved from death. This miracle caused the nobleman to believe as did "his whole house" (John 4:53). This result came as a consequence of another adult-focused evangelistic effort.

Entire households were saved also as a result of Paul's ministry among the Gentiles. In Acts 16:15 Lydia and her household were saved. The same thing occurred at the house of Cornelius (Acts 10). Many other such experiences occurred with persons such as the Philippian jailer (Acts 16:31-34); Crispus (Acts 18:8); and Stephanas (1 Cor. 1:16). In view of these experiences, it seems that the adult strategy and its concomitant effect on households was the established pattern in New Testament evangelism. There can be no doubt about it—*evangelism is first and foremost an adult matter.*

6. Adult Evangelism Is the Essence of Church Growth

Although the Book of Acts is not actually a history of church growth, the numerous references to the growth of the early churches provide an exciting story of the results those churches achieved in their efforts to "make disciples." These accounts invariably show that the thrust of these churches was directed toward winning adults to Christ. In fact, Luke records the growth in terms of progress in reaching adults. In Acts 1:15 he noted that there were about one hundred and twenty disciples. In Acts 4:4 he reported on male response to the gospel: "Howbeit many of them which heard the word believed; and the number of *men* was about five thousand" (author's italics). In Acts 5:14, Luke affirms a wholesale turning to God on the part of adults: "And believers were the more added to the Lord, multitudes of *men* and *women*" (author's italics). Following the ministry of Philip in Samaria, Luke noted: "But when they believed . . . they were baptized, both *men* and *women*" (Acts 8:12, author's italics).

In other places in Acts, the reports seem to become almost routine and even abbreviated. They simply state that the Word of God spread and that multitudes of people, including many of the priests of Judah, were added to the Lord. When it is remembered that adults were the leaders in spreading the gospel, it is impossible to avoid the conclusion that reaching unsaved adults was the total strategy for church growth in the churches of the New Testament era. This fact should make adult evangelism the major principle in church growth methodology. Moreover, the evidence all points to the fact that church growth is nothing more or less than an adult evangelistic movement. Likewise, it is evident that what is generally referred to as "New Testament evangelism" is in reality *adult evangelism.* It also seems that beyond any reasonable doubt all other types of evangelism are a spin-off of adult evangelism. It is categorically certain that the early advance of the church across pagan lands was sparked by the flames of adult evangelism. And the holy fervor which sustained the movement was one adult witnessing to another adult in the power of the Holy Spirit.

The most basic concept in all church growth activities is the principle of adult-to-adult witnessing. This activity is the quintessence of God's strategy at work. This kind of evangelism is the very heartbeat of Christianity. It is the distinguishing mark of the Christian religion. It is the most direct of all Christian efforts to serve God. It is the explicit work of a church, and it is the one thing from which all church growth that lasts emerges.

When a church fails to reach and evangelize the adult generation, it is not honoring the New Testament strategy of church growth. When a church fails to win adults it loses its spiritual glow. When a church substitutes some other strategy, it will have to settle for second best because no other method has equaled the results that this strategy produces. It is axiomatic that *evangelism on all fronts waits on evangelism on the adult front.*

7. Adult Evangelism Is a Spiritual Necessity

When Jesus looked upon the multitudes, he responded with deep compassion. His response was based on their dire need and their tragic condition. The description of their condition leaves no doubt that they were adults. Jesus saw them as shepherdless sheep (not lambs) who were weary and faint from their aimless wanderings. He saw them as burdened and bowed down with the weight of their sin. He saw them as scattered and helpless because sin had taken its toll. Their needs were acute, and his compassion was real. These were adults who were spiritually destitute.

Today millions of contemporary adults are in the same dreadful condition. Their plight should arouse Christians to the same compassionate response which Jesus gave. The Bible describes their condition and sets out their position in graphic terms. For example, they are referred to as *lost*. This word implies a lack of purpose, a frantic search for meaning in life, a deep sense of disillusionment, a warped moral perspective, and a need for immediate salvation. The Bible refers to these lost adults as "servants of sin," for they are in spiritual bondage and have no freedom in Christ. These adults have "no peace" for they have no hope of any kind. They are "condemned . . . already." They are "dead . . . in trespasses and sins." Their eyes have been blinded by the "gods of this world" so that they do not realize their most desperate need is spiritual. Because they trust in human philosophies, material possessions, social acceptance, and good works, they seek in vain for real solutions to their problems. Yet, their search is to no avail. They are *lost*.

The gospel of Christ is the only hope for these millions of lost men and women. The churches have the message and the means to evangelize these people. Yet, many neglect to do so. Some churches try to substitute some easy way to evangelize, like specializing in child evangelism or youth evangelism. There is no question about children and youth being candidates for salvation. They can be saved and they need to be saved, but a church can not be a *genuine* church when it writes off the adult generation because adults are not easy to reach. Avoiding or even neglecting adult evangelism creates a spiritual anemia that plagues many churches. It generates weakness in all areas of church life. Worst of all it reduces the making of disciples to nurturing, if not to taking advantage of the young.

The early churches did not have an easy time winning adults to Christ. They were harassed by an ingrown religious system, they were oppressed by the military legions of Rome, and they were tormented by their own countrymen. But they evangelized adults, including many persons from these very groups. They not only won their own generation, but also they won their entire world to Christ. Even though thousands of Christian adults gave their lives in the process, they overcame all of the forces which persecuted them and tried to annihilate them.

It is unlikely that anyone could imagine, much less describe, the impact that would be made on the world today if churches would take seriously the challenge of an unevangelized generation of adults. Millions of adults would find the new life in Christ which is described as "more abundant." Millions of adult lives now being wasted would become committed to the service of God. Innumerable homes on the brink of destruction would be turned into outposts for Christian witnessing. Thousands of struggling churches would become revitalized and strong in their stand for Christ. Churches that are handicapped by a lack of workers would find their leadership ranks swollen with new recruits. Churches harassed by meager resources would have enough and more than enough resources to spare for world missions. The moral climate of the world would be greatly improved, if not recreated. None of these things are the real purpose of evangelism, but they are magnificent fringe benefits which come as a result of adult evangelism.

The love of God, the sacrifice of Jesus, the mission of the church, and the tragic condition of lost adults all focus on one monumental truth: *reaching and winning unsaved adults is the only strategy that produces significant and lasting church growth.* And that truth is the reason there is no challenge in Christendom so vast in scope, so far-reaching in its influence, and so promising in its potential.

Part 2

The Sunday School Dynamics in Church Growth

5

Providing the Structure
for Growth

With the possible exception of the jellyfish it seems that every organism—living body—requires a supporting structure. As a living body, the church requires such a structure. That structure is the Sunday School. Properly conceived, appropriately organized, and effectively administered, the Sunday School is unquestionably the most significant factor in church growth. In fact, the Sunday School has no peer in church growth. It is all but axiomatic that "as goes the Sunday School, so goes the church."

Because of its unusual nature, its singular functions, and its dynamic utility, the Sunday School plays an increasingly important role in the total ministry of a church. In almost every way the Sunday School is congenerous with its church. This unique union of natures between the Sunday School and church grows out of the fact that *the Sunday School is the church structuring itself to carry out the Great Commission in the local community.* Although some Sunday Schools, and even some churches, do not seem to realize it, *the Sunday School is not a separate entity from the church.* The Sunday School has no life of its own. It is of the church, by the church, and for the church. By definition, *the Sunday School is the church* (1) showing its compassion by *reaching out to people*; (2) proclaiming its message by *engaging its members and prospects in life-changing Bible study*; (3) fulfilling its Commission by *winning persons to Christ and church*

83

membership; and (4) expressing its nature by *involving its members in the life and work of the church.*

Because of these unique interrelationships, the Sunday School has essentially the same reasons for existence, the same sense of mission, the same essential message, the same basic responsibilities, the same priority goals, and the same motivational interests as the church. These facts do not mean that the Sunday School and the church are exactly the same. The church is more than the Sunday School. However, all there is of the Sunday School is the church.

These important concepts point up the reasons why the Sunday School is not in competition with the church. A competitive relationship would in every way be self-defeating. These same concepts emphasize the fact that a church should never look condescendingly upon its Sunday School, for to do so would be to indulge in self-hatred. In this kind of relationship, *two can be one*, and *one can be two*; but *two cannot be two* without the negation of both. Without question, the church is the divine organism, but the Sunday School is a medium through which the organism well expresses its nature. In the contemporary world the Sunday School is the *basic structure* which the church assumes so that it can accomplish its mission effectively.

This concept of the interdependent relationships between a church and its Sunday School is not only theologically sound, it is philosophically defensible. Furthermore, it is essential to the proper understanding of the cause-and-effect connection between *Sunday School outreach* and *church growth.*

Webster's New Collegiate Dictionary defines *structure* as "something made up of independent parts in a definite pattern of organization." This definition is an exact description of the foregoing conceptualizations of Sunday School and church relationships. It is from this perspective that this book takes its stance. And it is from this perspective that a church and its Sunday School become the parts of a whole which enables the union to produce stable and sustained church growth.

It almost appears to be simplistic to say that church growth requires a stable structure. Nevertheless, it *does* require structure. And, it is distressing to realize how many church leaders and members seem to have a negative attitude toward structure and organization when both of these matters are so often seen in divine intelligence.

The place of structure needs to be emphasized because it is generally neglected in church-growth literature. The frequent insistence on a multiplicity of principles, laws, methods, and skills to produce growth inadvertently leaves the impression, "do it this way and you will grow like we have." These technical aspects of church growth are important and have their place, yet, without a supporting structure all growth eventually slows and fades away. At the risk of seeming to fall into the same type of entrapment, it seems necessary to make a strong case for structure. Nevertheless, it is quite impossible for any organism to grow beyond the limits of what its structure can support. And church growth always results in a need for additional structure. More precisely, structure is required before growth can be added to the organism. Furthermore, the conviction that the Sunday School when properly organized and functioning is the ideal structure for long-term and sustained church growth, is based on the composite experience of churches over several decades. The fact that churches fail to grow because they have inadequate structure seems to be an inescapable conclusion.

1. The Sunday School Structure Is Compatible with Growth

The Sunday School did not originate in church growth—or in the church at all, for that matter. Its earliest purpose was to provide schooling on Sunday for children who had no opportunity for formal learning. There were no public schools when the Sunday School was born. The Sunday School was simply a makeshift method for teaching unfortunate children to read and write. Sunday was used for the effort because it was the only day the children did not have to work in the shops and factories. The

English Sunday School, which was popularized by Robert Raikes, used mothers in various communities to teach reading and writing. These mothers were paid for their work. It was William Fox who introduced the idea of volunteer teachers and the use of the Bible. The Bible was the only book available on a scale large enough to be used as a text. These innovations made by Fox attracted the attention of Raikes, and the two men worked together to use the Bible as a basis for providing Sunday instruction in reading and writing.

It was in America, however, not in England, that the Sunday School flowered and came into full bloom. There are records which support the establishment of a Sunday School in Savannah, Georgia, in 1736. By 1740 there were several other Sunday Schools scattered along the Eastern seaboard. These schools were independent efforts, for it was not until about 1825 that churches began to realize that the Sunday School was compatible with the church. In 1875, after the Sunday School had "moved in" with the church, the rapid growth of both the Sunday School and the church began to occur. Growth of the Sunday School brought the need for more structure to handle the growth. In a short time the idea of age-group departments emerged to give the Sunday School more flexibility. This development soon brought into existence department-oriented buildings and created a need for uniform curriculum materials. Eventually graded curricula made their appearance. As these changes in Sunday School work began to develop, rapid growth added a new impetus to church life.

The above developments marked the beginning of a whole new epoch in church history. In addition to the rapid growth of Sunday Schools and churches, there was the emergence of programs of religious education, the development of an entirely new type of church building, a more effective medium for evangelism, the formation of principles and methods which produce church growth on a continuing basis, and the introduction of a new megachurch mentality. For these and other developments, it is crystal clear that the Sunday School has proven to be not only compatible with church growth, but essentially responsible for it and the concomitant developments in many aspects of church life.

To be sure, all churches and denominations did not profit equally from the new patterns of growth. These exceptions, however, only serve to underscore the difference a good Sunday School can make in the growth and development of a church. Today some churches and denominations are not enjoying the resurgence of growth which the Sunday School can make possible. These differences support the view that churches and leaders are different and that growth results are related to both the methods and skills of leaders. Perhaps more significantly, some churches and leaders do not desire unusual church growth.

Many churches still have the same Sunday School structure that they have had for several decades, and some churches have even less than before. A static or declining structure is certain to stop church growth. National and local demographics are never static. Therefore, the Sunday School organizational structure must be kept dynamic and flexible so that it is always synchronized with the current population. Provision of the past is not necessarily the best organizational pattern for the present. There is probably no existing organization that is exactly in harmony with the current needs and possibilities of any given church. This situation means that updating, adjusting, and enlarging of the Sunday School structure are imperative in most churches. If growth has stopped or if decline has set in, there is no question about the need for a thorough study of the structure. The first thing to suspect in nongrowing situations is structural deficiency.

At the present time most Sunday Schools are structured for the so-called "typical" American family of the past generation. Wherever this condition exists, an organizational metamorphosis is needed. It is virtually impossible to reach many types of persons until the Sunday School structure offers special provision for persons not now being reached. For example, additional provision needs to be made for the rapidly growing number of senior adults. The same is true for single adults and for preschoolers. There are numerous special outreach opportunities in connection with the handicapped, the retarded, the blind, the deaf, and the homebound. There are many challenges in the ethnic, bilingual, and language groups, but they all require additional structure not presently available in the majority of churches.

How a church structures its Sunday School speaks "loud and clear" to unreached persons. It can say, "We want you," and it can just as clearly say, "We don't want you" if the structure needed to reach persons is nonexistent. The unvarnished truth is that a Sunday School cannot grow until its organizational structure conforms to its potential. Fortunately, structure can be readily changed when the leaders help the people want to grow. The fact that structure can be readily modified, enlarged, and updated is what makes it so thoroughly compatible with church growth.

2. The Sunday School Structure Provides for All Available Persons

Actually not every Sunday School structure does provide for every person available to the Sunday School. However, the capability of providing for all persons is inherent in the nature of the Sunday School. It is an ideal that every Sunday School can achieve. It is a potential toward which every Sunday School should be working.

The initial step in providing for all persons is to discover exactly who should belong to the Sunday School. This information is most important. When it is not available, most Sunday School leaders resort to thinking in vague terms about provision. They think of Sunday School prospects as "all church members," "people who like our program," "our kind of folk," and even the impossible "everybody." Provision that is suitable and practical cannot be made on such a basis. The concepts are too ill-defined and all-inclusive to be useful. A Sunday School must know exactly who needs to be reached. The pertinent information about each prospective member should be gathered, kept current, and made available to teams for cultivation and enlistment visitation. The value of this kind of information cannot be overestimated. It is essential to organizational planning and administrative effectiveness. It is the kind of information that is essential for valid decision making. It is the substance from which attractive and dynamic structures are made.

Although the membership of a Sunday School is ideally all-inclusive, the structural units provided actually delineate who is wanted and eventually determine exactly who will be reached. This result strongly implies that when a church over a long period of time fails to enlarge and improve its structure, it is admitting that it does not intend to reach people and in effect is saying to its constituency, "We really don't want you."

It is quite unlikely that any church can provide at one time all of the Sunday School organization it needs or wants. This problem is most generally related to the lack of building space and a shortage of leaders. The solution to the problem lies in a periodic evaluation of the organization and a restructuring or enlargement of the provision. Every organizational enlargement makes possible a further enlargement at a later date. And, with the goal of providing for all available persons ever in view, a Sunday School can be dynamically moving its structure toward a realistic level of attainment. At the same time the church will be saying to its constituency, "We are providing for you because we want you." In this way the church will be able to avoid the inference, "We have nothing for you because we do not actually want you."

When a church relies solely on human intelligence, it will wait until new people attend and then seek to make provision for them. Divine wisdom, however, says, "Enlarge the place of thy tent, and let them stretch forth the curtains of thine habitations: spare not, lengthen thy cords, and strengthen thy stakes" (Isa. 54:2). In more contemporary terms this concept says that enlarged provision must *precede* outreach and growth.

3. The Sunday School Structure Facilitates Assignments for Growth

The lack of specificity in reaching persons is probably the greatest hindrance to Sunday School outreach and church growth. The "y'all come," "everybody bring someone," and "visitors are welcome" clichés are only superficial evidences of a vague uneasiness about failure to reach out to "win the world to Christ."

It is a rare person who actually cares for a lost *world*. Caring for a "world" is too impersonal, too impractical, and too impressionistic. Human beings do not care for "worlds." They care for other human beings, but only for other persons whom they actually know. Caring grows out of empathy. Empathy grows out of concern. Concern grows out of personal knowledge. Knowledge grows out of association. Association grows out of efforts to reach an individual. In other words, caring is a particularized response to a specific individual.

The outreach process is normally the work of the Sunday School. Why is this statement true? Because the Sunday School is the only approach a church has for making everyone in the community the responsibility of someone in the church. This definitive responsibility is exceedingly important. It is highly specific. Potentially it is the church's answer to the many problems involved in reaching a world, a state, a country, a city, or even a community for Christ.

Because everybody's business is nobody's business, intangibleness is the problem in Sunday School outreach, just as it is in all approaches to church growth. Therefore, making nobody's business become somebody's business is a real challenge.

It must become somebody's business to get it done. Because the Sunday School organization is the nearest thing a church has to "everybody," it seems logical that the Sunday School be designated as the "somebody" to get outreach done. Actually, the Sunday School is the only specific *people-reaching* organization a church has. All other programs and organizations, vital as they are, have functions that are almost totally focused on people who have already been reached. These organizations sometimes reach people through their *specialties*, but their priorities are on various aspects of discipling, not on outreach. It should never be overlooked that when a Sunday School is enrolling people it is not just serving its own ends. It is also working for all other organizations and interests of the church as a whole.

To serve the needs of the entire church, Sunday School membership should include all persons: unsaved persons, unaffiliated persons, members of the church, and nonparticipating adherents to other churches and religions. Sunday School membership is truly comprehensive and extensive. This open membership ideal is the very first step in making a specific approach to growth. *Because no one is excluded, everyone is included.* The Sunday School is not only designed to reach everyone; it is able to do so by establishing contact, developing relationships, involving persons in Sunday School activities, and cultivating readiness for salvation. Furthermore, a Sunday School can carry on these reaching activities on a sustained and indefinite basis.

By its approach to grading and grouping, a Sunday School can permanently assign prospects to appropriate departments and classes so that continuing interest in a given prospective member is possible. This continuity is a valuable way to show that a church is concerned about specific persons rather than in the pursuit of potential members.

Within these distinctive concepts there is no significant difference between Sunday School outreach and church growth.

Sunday School outreach is simply the way a church makes a specific assignment for reaching people and expressing its innate need to grow.

4. The Sunday School Structure Provides Leadership for Growth

The ultimate success or failure of any human enterprise rests in the hands of the leaders. In the matter of church growth, the leadership factor is exceedingly critical because the Sunday School workers determine not only the size of the Sunday School but the eventual growth of the church as well. This conclusion is based on the fact that a properly organized Sunday School would have a number of leaders equal to about 10 percent of the total enrollment and about 5 percent of the church membership. All of these leaders have some facet of responsibility for reaching people both as a Sunday School worker and as a Christian. Also, many of these workers have an outreach assignment in their position title. Therefore, a church has in its Sunday School a large corps of "outreachers." There is a *general* outreach director, *department* outreach leaders, and in the adult classes there are both *class* outreach leaders and *group* leaders. These persons, when properly trained, mobilized, and motivated have unusual potential for providing a high level of Sunday School and church growth.

Beyond question, the most significant development in contemporary church life is the Sunday School as the agency for outreach and the medium of church growth. Likely the most important aspect of Sunday School effectiveness in outreach and growth is the abundance of volunteer leaders it can muster for the task.

5. The Sunday School Structure Personalizes Church Growth Efforts

Making a diligent effort to personalize all outreach efforts is the great challenge in church growth. In a culture in which numbers are all but synonymous with names, identification is subordinate to identity, and computer dossiers are equivalent to personal knowledge, almost any effort that seeks to personalize its work will be successful. This circumstance makes a personal visit so much better than a telephone call and a telephone call so much better than any written communication.

The attitude of a church toward persons is extremely important. If a church sees unreached persons only as prospective members, its outreach will be less than personal. If a church views unsaved individuals primarily as evangelistic possibilities, its methodology will be oriented to the masses rather than to individuals. If a church thinks of people as a means for church growth, rather than as persons in desperate need, there will be a noticeable failure to grow.

A *world* will not likely be brought to Christ, a *country* will not be evangelized, a *state* will not become Christian, and a *community* will not become churched. *Individuals* are brought to Christ one at a time. Salvation is not a mass movement. Reaching people is a personal matter. Jesus *wept* over the multitudes, but he *reached out* to individuals. His ministry was widespread but it was characterized by the personal touch. His methods were varied, but his approach was person centered.

It is difficult for a church to think in terms of individuals, but it can develop an individualized methodology by using its Sunday School properly. The Sunday School organization is designed to discover *individuals* who need Christ, to cultivate *persons* who are slow to respond, and to witness *individually* to unsaved *persons*.

The Sunday School structure with its age-group organization can make outreach visitation a peer-to-peer personal expression of Christ's love. The Sunday School can in every way become a person-minded ministry when it remembers that "nothing is worth the building that does not build the person." A church will have no problem with means and ends in its growth activities when it remembers that people as individuals are the ends while outreach and growth are simply the means.

6. The Sunday School Structure
Produces Maximum Involvement in Growth Activities

A planned program of outreach visitation is absolutely essential if a church is to express its concern for the *people* in its community. A matter of such importance requires specific and effective leadership. Obviously, the pastor, even when aided by a competent staff, can never maintain the intimate contacts necessary to reaching persons. The very nature of outreach requires the maximum involvement of the church members in a large variety of people-reaching activities.

In its Sunday School organization a church has at its command a wealth of outreach resources. The Sunday School not only "employs" the largest number of lay leaders, but specific leaders who have the essential spiritual skills required for outreach. These persons, more than any other group, can put Christianity into practice by developing a personal interest in a large number of unreached persons all at one time. They can create and express a genuine caring, compassionate concern for these people. They can maintain a continuing relationship long enough to maximize the impact of the church on the "outside world." Sunday School workers are able to use a great variety of growth methods and skills on a simultaneous basis. They can minister to the needs of the persons they are cultivating and at the same time witness to all of those who are responsive.

In addition to the Sunday School leaders, there are many members of adult classes who can be enlisted to help in various growth activities. These members generally have a feeling of need to be involved, but they need guidance and encouragement. Many of them also have personal contacts where they work and live that the regular visitation program would rarely touch. There is an all but unlimited potential for growth in the enlistment, guidance, and use of the adult class members. This group of people constitutes the church's most significant pool of untapped resources for growth. And it is readily available through the Sunday School organization.

7. The Sunday School Is a Continuing and Stable Force for Growth

Permanent growth is not an instantaneous accomplishment. It is slow and difficult work. It requires a long-term approach. Above all, growth activities require a continuing and stable structure if they are to be effective. Growth is not a seasonal emphasis, a "sometimes" thing to do. It is an essential all-the-time task that requires a strong supporting organization.

Because the Sunday School is organized on the age basis, it effectively distributes *continuing* responsibility for every potential member. Because the Sunday School is organized for outreach, it has a *stable* and *dependable* working force that is on the job at all times. Because the Sunday School teaches the Bible, its members are *constantly* aware of the plight of lost people. Because the Sunday School is the way the church structures itself for outreach, the church has a built-in, constant, ongoing expression of its concern for people. And it already has a unique organization which can provide a sustained program of outreach, evangelism, and growth.

6

Penetrating the Community for Growth

When Jesus established his church, he gave it a twofold mission: (1) the *ultimate penetration* of the entire world; and (2) the *immediate permeation* of Jerusalem. These two goals were to be realized by an endless pervasion of all inhabited areas between Jerusalem and the remainder of the world. God's instrument for this mission then and now is the church. Three methods are to be used: (1) the preaching of the gospel; (2) the teaching of the Scriptures; and (3) the outreach of the Christians.

From its inception the church has been indigenous to its context, flexible in its institutional expression, and dynamic in its structures. These magnificent characteristics have enabled the church to adjust and adapt to meet the needs of time and place. This indigenous quality has also produced a great variety of church types and church programs. However, there seems to be one overall characteristic of all growing churches—the ability to penetrate the church community.

The first church seemed to take two basic approaches to the penetration of Jerusalem. It used the Temple area for *mass meetings of an evangelistic nature,* and it used the homes of people for *small-group worship and spiritual growth activities.* It is difficult, if not impossible, to determine whether these approaches had theological significance or were simply pragmatic necessities because of the lack of any buildings for church purposes. These two approaches may very well have been the

97

visible evidence of a definite and well-planned strategy for penetrating the community.

It seems highly significant that contemporary churches use these same basic approaches. The church sanctuary provides for the corporate activities, and the Sunday School with its graded organization, provides the small group and personalized settings for teaching and reaching activities. Both of these groupings complement and supplement each other. They are both essential to the full expression of the life in the community of faith.

Even without church buildings the early churches functioned as corporate institutions. They came together as a *gathered community (ekklēsia)* to *worship, learn,* and *relate* to each other. They dispersed, and became a *scattered community* on a mission of *preaching, teaching, witnessing,* and *outreach.* The dispersed activities undoubtedly were direct acts of obedience to Christ's injunction, "Go ye." These activities resulted in a penetration of Jerusalem with a witness to Christ and a person-to-person sharing of the gospel message.

If contemporary churches are to penetrate their respective communities, they need much more than a perfunctory "Come ye" approach to outreach. They must learn to communicate through the channels of the culture in which the church is housed, and they must be able to speak to the spiritual needs of individuals as well as to the public at large. This style of communication certainly includes preaching and teaching. These activities are significant means of communication with persons who *come to the church.* Nevertheless, a church dares not limit its communication to those methods if it hopes to penetrate its community for Christ. The "everywhere" technique of the early churches must be added to the "somewhere" technique of present-day churches.

Although a few churches experience numerical increase without any obvious penetration activities, it is highly doubtful that such churches are growing *in proportion to their potential.* Churches in growing communities may produce the appearance of growth while making no appreciable impact on the unreached community. From this viewpoint, church growth is only relative. It is generated by natural causes rather than by deliberate obedience to Christ's commands.

Because the Sunday School is *the church structuring itself for outreach and growth,* it is the most effective means of penetration. It is already organized and available for the task. It needs only to be mobilized and motivated. Several approaches are possible.

1. Build an Identity with the Community

Although a church is *in* the world, it is not *of* the world. On the other hand, a church exists in a particular locality to bear witness to that specific community. If there is no vital relationship between a church and its community, there is little likelihood of any meaningful ministry to the unchurched people or anything more than internal church growth through the conversion of family members.

A community always has an image of what it perceives any given church to be, and a feeling of what that church ought to be like. These two perceptions are frequently different from the perception of the church members. A church and community meeting of the minds is needed when these differing viewpoints exist. It is essential that a church seek to become compatible with its community and relate to it in a positive and supportive manner. No church can afford to become introverted or withdrawn from its own culture. A church should never separate itself from the secular world. It must not become a *society of the select.* If a church is to perform its mission adequately, it must be both *indigenous* to the community and appropriately identified with it.

To identify with its community, a church needs to have a degree of sameness in purpose, a mutuality of overall concerns, and an attitude of helpfulness in serving the best interests of the community. A church should consider itself as the major contributor to the wholesomeness of the community. These goals and attitudes are in the best interest of the church. They do not require or even entertain the idea of compromise. They are the natural outgrowth of a sincere desire to be on mission for God.

The first church of Jerusalem was judged by its community to have an acceptable identity for it is written that they were "praising God, and *having favour with all the people*" (author's italics, Acts 2:47a). The Greek word translated *favour* means graciousness in manner and action. It implies a spiritual influence upon the heart and reflection in the life of the persons involved. It results in being happy and acceptable to other people.

A church identifies with its community in a variety of ways. However, the community judges a church primarily on the obvious basis of attendance, especially the Sunday School attendance. Sunday School growth is easily observed, and it creates interest and excitement.

When a Sunday School has an active visitation program to the unreached, it is demonstrating its concern for people, especially the people in the church community. Even those persons who belong to other churches respond favorably to a church that tries to enlist new people in Sunday School.

When the outreach work of the Sunday School is supported by loving, personal ministries to persons in the community, the church is not only identifying with the special needs of the community, but the community accepts these efforts as evidence of a caring congregation. The extension activities of the Sunday School such as the Vacation Bible School, work with the homebound, Backyard Bible Clubs, and fellowship Bible classes are especially impressive to a church community.

Along with the functional contributions to the community, a Sunday School should make some direct *intentional* efforts to win the confidence and respect of its community. Even a casual research project will identify special needs and interests to which the Sunday School can respond. The fact that it makes an effort will, in itself, communicate sincere concern for, and commitment to, the community.

2. Search for Unreached Persons

Any Sunday School that fails to reach out has lost its reason for existence. And any Sunday School that fails to permeate its community with a variety of people-seeking activities is already in a state of decline even though through internal or biological growth it may be experiencing an increase in enrollment and attendance. Seeking unreached persons is required by both the nature and purpose of the Sunday School, regardless of how strongly it may be committed to Bible teaching. As a matter of fact, Bible teaching itself provides a large part of the motivation for outreach.

When a Sunday School is determined to penetrate its community, it will find itself actively engaged in discovering and enrolling every unreached person possible. This means that *all* persons will be included in the search. There will be no groups, classes, races, social levels, cultural, or ethnic distinctions made. Prospective Sunday School members have only one qualifying distinction—they are presently *unreached*.

Churches and Sunday School leaders should realize that practically every community is increasingly pluralistic. This fact ought to challenge churches to be Christian enough to use every means available to reach every person possible, regardless of their national origin or station in life. This attitude is inherent in the Great Commission. Reaching all kinds of people is the mission of the church. Reaching all persons in the community is the *responsibility* of the Sunday School. It is also the mission task of the Christian.

Searching for unreached persons is not only essential to the growth of the Sunday School, it is the very lifeline of the church. Searching is utterly important to everything a Sunday School does to reflect its concern for people. And everything a church does should be evaluated in terms of its contribution to reaching people.

Searching for people is difficult in some types of communities, but there is no better way to penetrate a community. *Searching* is an intentional approach to penetration. *Searching* is an essential factor in church growth. *Searching* is a continual, never-ending function of a growing Sunday School. *Searching* is a vital and viable part of a church program—if the church has any desire to grow.

3. Cultivate Slow-to-Respond Persons

In the world of agriculture, cultivation is as important to a growing crop as fertilizer and water. In reaching a community for Christ the *cultivation* of persons who are slow to respond is as essential as preaching and praying. Although the very word *cultivation* turns some aggressive Christians livid, it is a valid concept. It is valid simply because most of the quick-to-respond persons have already been reached. However, there is a much better reason for cultivating persons. Cultivation is theologically sound. The Jerusalem church used it constantly. Luke makes the record clear: "And *every day* in the temple and *at home* they did not cease teaching and preaching" (Acts 5:42, RSV, author's italics). This statement indicates person-to-person cultivation. In a short time, about three years following Pentecost, the first church had filled Jerusalem with converts to Christ. This development could not have come with only a hard-hitting, one-time witness, even if it were highly manipulative. These early Christians went *repeatedly into the homes of the people to cultivate their interest*. This action was *fellowship evangelism*. There was far too much prejudice, disbelief, and antagonism for every contact to produce a convert. Cultivation was an absolute essential.

The very act of reaching for prospective members is a basic sort of evangelism. When it is followed up by identifying persons who are found, making use of the information gained, and visiting repeatedly to establish a teaching and witnessing relationship, it *is* evangelism both in process and in fact. Furthermore, it is generally more productive than a more aggressive approach that is "pushy" and coercing.

In any effort to penetrate a community for Christ, a loving, friendly, cultivative approach will produce a greater impact than many mass evangelism approaches. This statement is especially true if the lasting efforts, such as the assimilation of the converts into a church, are taken into account.

There are several reasons why the Sunday School is the ideal cultivation instrument. It is responsible for the outreach task of the church. It is organized on an age-level basis which makes possible a continuing relationship both during and after the cultivation period. The Sunday School is ideal for cultivation also because it has the best outreach people in its organization. Again, it has, or should have, a well-planned and effective visitation program. In the adult area there is an extensive organization on both the department and class levels that is designed especially for reaching out to people. This organization provides a *continuing cultivation capability.* It can *stay in touch* with all unreached adults. The adult organization also includes a *constant contact competency.* And equally important is the Sunday School's ability to *involve in cultivation activities more people than any other organizational approach.* These Sunday School potentialities are invaluable in cultivating persons who need to be reached for Bible study, Christ, and church membership.

4. Provide Outreach Bible Study Opportunities

The New Testament church continually devoted itself to the "teaching of the apostles" (Acts 2:42, Williams). This intensive Bible teaching was a direct response to Christ's command to teach them "to observe all things whatsoever I have commanded you" (Matt. 28:20). Although this teaching was doctrinally based, it was much more than an indoctrination course for new converts. It was designed for outreach. It had a community impact objective. In its outreach application the teaching program of the early church took an "apologetic" form. The term *apologetic* is not to be confused with an apology; rather it is technical in nature. It involves an *explanation* of the gospel, a *witness* to the Old Testament teachings about Christ, and an *authentication* of the Christian faith. An apologetic was a positive and assertive approach to Bible teaching which the Holy Spirit used to bring conviction and conversion. It should not be overlooked that those early proclaimers of the truth used a didactic approach in all of the messages recorded in the Scriptures.

From the very beginning of the church, Bible teaching has played a major role in outreach and evangelism. This vital activity grows out of the fact that New Testament Christianity has always been concerned with reaching people to teach them the Bible. Outreach is the *mission* of the church, and *teaching* is the method. Outreach requires Bible teaching, and Bible teaching prompts outreach. There is a singular cause-and-effect relationship between the two activities. This relationship is the reason why reaching and teaching are always visible in authentic church growth. And this relationship is also the reason why Bible teaching has no peer in all areas of church growth. Teaching is suitable to any situation. It is adaptable to any setting. And it is both a natural and a supernatural approach to the penetration of a community.

There are several short-term and long-term Bible teaching projects which are suitable for penetration.

● Vacation Bible Schools, both at the church building and in temporary quarters throughout a community, are extremely important outreach projects. Many churches and missions have had their origin in a Vacation Bible School, and many communities have first become aware of a caring church through these schools.

• Backyard Bible Clubs are essentially a mini Bible School. They are brief projects of one to five days for about an hour and a half each session. Bible Clubs may be conducted not only in backyards, but in carports, shaded areas, on patios, playgrounds, in parks, and almost any available space. The Backyard Bible Club is primarily for children, but often a class for mothers is a possibility.

• Bible study fellowships in the homes are a viable method of penetration. These study groups should be carefully planned and church sponsored if they are to produce the best results.

• Branch or mission Sunday Schools are excellent approaches to penetration in many communities.

• Bible-centered recreation projects are quite useful in penetrating certain types of communities.

• Language Bible study groups which provide Bible teaching in an ethnic language often develop into missions and churches. Instruction in how to speak, read, and write in English is also a good approach in many communities.

• Newcomer Bible study at the church building is a useful approach to some communities. The pastor or a qualified lay person may teach the Scriptures from a get-acquainted stance. These classes generally are held on a lunchtime schedule one day per week.

5. Witness to Responsive Persons

When Jesus sent his apostles out to visit-witness, they did not go with a prospect card in hand to deliver a canned evangelistic sales pitch. They were not looking for specific persons. Their target group on this occasion was *any person who was responsive*. The apostles simply shared the good news and witnessed to those who responded.

If a church is to penetrate a community effectively, it will need some type of witnessing program. There are many possible approaches. Perhaps a plan patterned after the one Jesus used with the apostles would be useful. If the event were organized as

"Operation Permeate," for example, it could have a wide appeal to the church. All of the Sunday School leaders and the adult members are a ready-made witnessing team. Such a large group of persons could readily spread out through a community to witness to responsive persons. It would even be possible to invite these persons to a home in the area for a fellowship with other persons who are members of the church, along with the pastor.

In planning and conducting community witnessing projects, some guidelines may be helpful:

(1) Always include and involve the Sunday School forces.

(2) Assess the community situation carefully.

(3) Plan to witness in a saturation manner.

(4) Hold a briefing meeting to acquaint the workers with the plans and procedures.

(5) Train the workers to witness in a natural, realistic manner that is suitable to the community.

Permeating a community with the gospel is not an easy task, but it is not as difficult as many persons suppose. The main problem is having enough people to do the work. Fortunately, the Sunday School provides a large reservior of witnesses. It is not only the largest group a church has, but it is also the best group for the task. It is unnecessary and unwise to ignore this available resource and give time and effort to enlist, train, and motivate other persons to do what the Sunday School is already designed to do. If the Sunday School is not witnessing, leaders can spend the time getting them prepared and involved. That time and effort will be highly productive.

6. Minister to the Special Needs of Persons

There is an "incarnational" principle in theology which speaks to the integrity of one's faith. James, the pastor of the Jerusalem church, spoke to this matter when he wrote: "Surely you can see that faith was at work in his actions, and that by these actions the integrity of his faith was fully proved" (James 2:22, NEB). In less technical language, this principle means that a person really believes what he practices. When God became incarnate in Christ, divine love came in the flesh. As love incarnate, Jesus ministered uniquely to the needs of persons. He also taught that when Christians minister to others they are, in effect, ministering to him. (See Matt. 25:34-40.) Persons who belong to Christ are actually responding to Christ in their ministry to others—if they minister in his name and in his Spirit. In this way the world understands Christ because it sees him in the loving ministry to Christians.

Christianity is much more than ministering to personal needs. However, the integrity of one's faith is readily seen in the way one responds to need, especially in times of crisis. Although ministries do not produce faith, faith apart from ministry is insipid, if not extinct.

Every community is overrun with need, not only special need, but excruciating need of every kind. And every community is in effect saying to the churches "show me your faith." This situation is incongruous especially when it is remembered that many churches are dying simply because they have served themselves so long that it seems pointless to continue.

Personal and family crises are an opportune time to communicate the love of God, to share the gospel of Christ, to be an incarnation of the Christian faith. It is in a time of crisis that we best communicate the meaning of faith and demonstrate what Christ really means. Arthur Flake, in a handwritten letter to the author, once shared this appropriate quotation: "All occasions invite his mercies and all times are his seasons."

Real ministry, especially in an effort to penetrate a community, is difficult to "program." Therefore, most ministry is a response rather than a deliberate act. Nevertheless, ministry is an assignment of the Sunday School and a privilege of Sunday School leaders and members. It offers an opportunity to serve as one would like to be served. It provides a setting for practicing what Jesus practiced. It gives a significant opening to demonstrate Christian love.

When ministry is taken seriously, it will bless persons, enrich families, improve communities, and give viable witness to Christ before a needy world. Ministry is indeed the "inasmuch" evidence of genuine faith as well as the most potent human factor in penetrating a community for Christ.

7

Teaching the Bible
for Growth

Both directly and indirectly the Sunday School makes many vital contributions to the church. Few, if any, of these contributions surpass the impact that Bible teaching has on the growth of a church. This conclusion is based on the assumption that the Bible is the preeminent textbook of the Sunday School. The conclusion also assumes that the quality of teaching and the type of study are both conducive to evangelism, discipleship, and church edification.

On the surface, the relationship between Bible teaching and church growth may not seem obvious. This seeming lack of relational recognition probably grows out of the fact that the Bible does not speak directly to a connection between Bible teaching and church growth. However, the Bible plays a very important role in a variety of relationships to which it does not speak manifestly. As a case in point, recall that the Bible often portrays God as reaching out to men through other men, yet it does not state that concept forthrightly. This truth-by-implication principle is valid. It means, however, that if an individual is to discover the efficacy of the Bible in many important areas, one must move from seeking a simple or direct statement of concept in all cases to a careful consideration of the intent of numerous experiences which the Bible records. The reality of this principle is illustrated in Luke's statement, "and the word of God increased; and the number of the disciples multiplied" (Acts

6:7a). Although this passage does not say that Bible teaching produced church growth, that meaning is clearly implied. This expansive quality of the Bible is one of the significant reasons for its being so much more than mere dogma, moral teachings, or even divine directives. Even by its implications the truths of the Bible are magnificent beyond description.

Because the Sunday School is committed to Bible teaching and outreach, it is the most influential factor in church growth. And, because the Bible is inspired, it exerts a profound influence on the very existence of the church. Moreover, the strength of the church, the dynamics of the congregational life, and the usefulness of the institution itself are all evidences of the impact of Bible teaching. As "the power of God" (Rom. 1:16), the Bible has the dynamic to produce church growth, the authority to guide church growth, and the motivation to generate church growth. These potentialities give credence to the belief that a Sunday School which teaches the Bible effectively will produce a vibrant and growing church. This growth power of Bible teaching is immense. The whole of church history is a substantiation of the influence of Bible teaching on church growth. Furthermore, this influence factor found in effective Bible teaching explains the stagnation and decline of churches which allow their Bible teaching program to deteriorate into a second-rate affair.

Many contemporary churches are discovering that Bible teaching in a strongly administered Sunday School plays the decisive role in the spiritual progress and numerical growth of their church. These important results stem from the fact that Bible teaching and Bible study are essential to both the effectiveness of individual Christians and the mission of a church. Nevertheless, it needs to be pointed out that the Sunday School approach to Bible teaching needs to be distinctively different from all other kinds of teaching. This difference is dictated by the difference in the text and the purpose of the teaching. Because the Bible is unique in its nature and inspired in its content, it cannot be taught like math, science, art, or any other such subject. As a matter of fact, the approach to Bible teaching in Sunday School should be quite different from every other type of Bible teaching, Bible study, and Bible learning. Failure to understand and observe this difference accounts for the unfortunate popular image of the Sunday School. A Sunday School teacher is sometimes seen as an inept lay person who stands before a class to bring the lesson for a group of members to enjoy. Although this image, inadequate as it is, represents the heritage out of which the Sunday School has grown, it can in no way be considered adequate for today. The Sunday School does indeed owe much to this primitive pattern, but it has much more to offer the people and the church.

If Sunday School Bible teaching is to be all it can become, it should focus on helping persons study the Bible in terms of the *biblical revelation*. The term *biblical revelation* should not be equated with the Book of Revelation even though that book is included in the concept of the biblical revelation. The words *biblical revelation* are simply a distinctive way to designate a special theological concept of the Bible. The concept refers to the manner in which the Bible is the written history of God's activity on behalf of man. It is God's own revealed record of what he has done to make it possible for man to know him and to live in fellowship with him. Therefore, the *content* of the revelation centers in God's personal disclosure of himself to man. In the Bible, God's personal revelation climaxes in Jesus Christ, and the message God has given is the gospel of Jesus Christ. Both God's revelation and God's message focus on God's Son who is the final and complete interpretation of the ultimate meaning of the Bible. Therefore, in a most singular fashion the Bible and Jesus Christ are inseparably united. They are bound together in a mystical union of the written Word and the living Word. The purpose of this union is to perfectly communicate God's immeasurable love for man.

Conceptually, the term *biblical revelation* also implies a special kind of Bible teaching. It refers to a style of teaching which concentrates on relating Bible truth to life. From this viewpoint, Bible teaching is concerned primarily with helping persons come to know Christ as Savior and Lord. This kind of teaching is also committed to helping persons grow in their capacity to be like Christ. In these ways, the relating-truth-to-life approach to Bible teaching is inherently more practical than academic. It is designed to help persons develop a comprehensive understanding of the Bible rather than to gain an exhaustive knowledge of it. When Bible teaching is focused on helping persons relate truth to life, they learn to cope with their problems in a Christlike manner rather than in mere human ways. Although the truth-to-life focus is concerned about the total person, guiding persons in their spiritual growth is more significant than meeting their physical, emotional, and intellectual deficiencies. It is also important to understand that the truth-to-life way of teaching is designed to complement preaching and never to compete with it. It features teaching as guiding, and learning as participation in the learning experience.

As a living message from the living God, the Bible is very deeply concerned with the immediate and ultimate spiritual needs of his creatures. He wants them to be redeemed. He wants them to be restored to his fellowship. And these same divine objectives are the concern of the biblical revelation and the Bible teaching aspect of the Sunday School. Finally, these are the same concerns which create the incomparable relationship between Bible teaching and church growth. An interpretation of this relationship follows.

1. Bible Teaching Communicates the Love of God

From the beginning to the end, God's great love is the central theme of the Bible. This special dimension of God's love was first revealed in his dealings with Adam and Eve after their willful disobedience in the Garden of Eden. The special quality of God's love is also evident throughout the Old Testament as God cared for his Chosen People. This love was demonstrated over and over again as God entered into human history through his mighty acts and his personal confrontations with man. The steadfastness of God's love is seen as he patiently guided the events of time with his own mighty hand. In many ways the Bible is the record of God moving toward man, reaching out to man, and bringing man to salvation.

God's redeeming love is expressed in his perfect provision for man's sin. The sacrificial systems of the Old Testament were simply a foreshadowing of the ultimate expression of God's love as he gave his own Son in death for the sins of the world. Although they were three separate events, the birth of Christ, the crucifixion of Christ, and the resurrection of Christ, all blend into one magnificent expression of God's all pervasive love for man. And the church exists to be God's continuing expression of his love through Jesus Christ. As the church reaches out to people and teaches them the Bible it is validating its own love for people and reflecting the beauty of God's special love.

As the outreach-teaching arm of the church, the Sunday School expresses in an organized way how the church responds to unreached persons. In teaching the matchless truths of the Bible, the Sunday School both interprets and illustrates the love of God for people. In the process of teaching and practicing God's love, the truth is demonstrated before the world. In this process, truth penetrates the mind, convicts the conscience, opens the heart, and illumines the will of persons who study the Scriptures. Persons who respond to these divine truths come to feel the constraining love of Christ. They learn to understand the extent of God's love, and they are able to respond in faith. As they continue to study the Bible they are able to comprehend what Paul really said when he noted: "God shows his love for us in that while we were yet sinners Christ died for us" (Rom. 5:8, RSV).

2. Bible Teaching Stimulates an Experiential Faith

Although salvation is rooted and grounded in God's grace, the Christian life is essentially a life of faith. It is based on faith in the historical Jesus; it is built on faith in the risen Christ. In some ways this faith is a simple kind of faith because it is primarily a matter of belief. It is an intellectual acceptance of certain facts. Belief accepts the factual testimony of history about Jesus Christ. It embraces as truth the events surrounding his birth, life, death, and resurrection. This belief assents to the biblical statement that "Christ died for our sins" (1 Cor. 15:3). Belief acknowledges that God's Son saves from sin and from its penalty.

In believing these foundational concepts of Christianity an individual is exercising a type of faith that is based on knowledge. Although this factual knowledge is true and essential, it is only the beginning point in real faith. There is much, much more to an authentic Christian faith.

There is a very special aspect to saving faith. Saving faith is experiential. An experiential faith has an element of belief, but there is the need for an emotional commitment to Christ. This commitment is not necessarily an emotional experience, but it is an emotional reality because it is a response of love for Christ. This love is implanted by the Holy Spirit and is accompanied by personal repentance for sin. If this love response is lacking, a person has only accepted a body of religious facts. He has not likely *experienced* a saving faith in Christ. A person can believe Christ died for all people. *Saving faith* is the realization: *he died for me.*

When a person actually experiences faith, one moves from knowing what one has believed to knowing in whom one has believed. This experiential faith can be evaluated. The evidence of a true faith experience is seen when the person makes progress in loving God with all one's heart and loving one's neighbor as one loves oneself.

There is likely no aspect of Sunday School teaching that needs or deserves more careful attention than the distinction between exposure *to* the truth and an experience *with* the truth. And, there is no greater satisfaction to be gained in teaching than that of leading class members from exposure to experience. Teachers need to be taught to see that helping persons experience faith requires a great deal more than sharing information from or about the Bible. This truism means that teaching must never be only content centered. If content is both the point to begin and the point to terminate teaching, then real learning will never occur unless it be by sheer accident. Bible truth must become both personal and practical if it is to be useful in the laboratory of living experience.

3. Bible Teaching Produces a Distinctive Commitment

The Christian *life* originates in a believing faith, but the Christian *experience* grows out of the trusting quality of one's faith. The genuiness of faith is best seen in the quality of one's commitment to Christ. Total commitment is the goal. And this kind of commitment means that the total person is voluntarily given over to the total control of Christ. Such a commitment is the real difference between the *beginning* of the Christian life and the *living* of the Christian life.

Although this total commitment is the ideal of the Christian life, it is not achieved by many persons. In some ways this shortcoming may be due to a lack of understanding of what is actually involved. Total commitment to Christ involves the intellect because it requires an unquestioning faith in God. Total commitment involves the physical powers in that it requires an unshrinking involvement in cooperative effort. Total commitment also involves the volitional strength because it calls for an unceasing surrender of the will to the Holy Spirit. This depth and quality of commitment is undoubtedly the most pressing need of this generation of Christians.

The growth and development of this type of commitment is not natural to life. It is a supernatural achievement of the Holy

Spirit in conjunction with a willing and yielded Christian. It requires an inner sensitivity to the Spirit of God, and it involves the right kind of nurture in the Christian community. These reasons strongly indicate the continuing need for regular Bible study in the company of other Christians who also are seeking a total commitment to Christ. Both the nurture and the company are provided by the Sunday School's Bible teaching ministry. In this environment the Christian has both the opportunity and the encouragement to grow in one's commitment. Furthermore, one finds opportunity to practice many of the attitudes and activities which will help one overcome the shallow, ineffective, and unproductive life-style of so many church people who seem to be "keeping up the forms of religion but not giving expression to its power" (2 Tim. 3:5, Williams). The movement toward total commitment is slow and sometimes discouraging, but it is greatly enhanced in an effective Sunday School Bible study situation.

4. Bible Teaching Instills Worthy Goals

The need for worthy goals, especially among God's people, has never been greater. Consequently, the need for a style of Bible teaching which lifts up worthy goals has never been more pronounced. In contemporary life there is a strong emphasis on goals. Individuals are taught to set personal, family, business, church, and even spiritual goals.

Granted, there is much to be said in favor of a goal-oriented life but there is also a real danger in this concept for Christians. The danger is that a Christian in pursuing his or her own goals, strategies, actions, and initiatives may overlook the fact that God already has a plan for him or her. To ignore this fact is to be presumptuous and arrogant. To fail to seek and find God's goals may also mean missing the best in life, for God's plans are always superior.

For the Christian there is something better than goals. There is a threefold integrating center around which one may build one's life. The Christian's integrating center begins with God's will. Living in that will is the ultimate Christian goal and the secret of a happy and successful life. There is also one's commitment to Christ which is the supreme loyalty in life for the Christian. And again, there is the indwelling presence of the Holy Spirit which is the energizing power in life. When this "tri-unity" of divine realities is properly understood and appropriately internalized into the Christian's approach to life, the world's standards of success are recognized as sinking sand. The Christian who seeks to build on them seems simple, if not foolish.

Discovering, understanding, and being willing to live in God's will, totally committed to Christ and empowered by the Spirit, requires genuine Bible study. The quality of Bible teaching is dramatically tested by the quality of the goals that learners adopt. When Christians assume that their lives belong only to themselves and feel that they are free to do as they please, they have either failed to learn or they have not had the right kind of Bible teaching.

5. Bible Teaching Magnifies the Christian Life-Style

Few, if any, subjects are treated more extensively in the New Testament than the uniqueness of the Christian style of living. To be sure, there is no formal statement of step-by-step Christian behavior. But there are numerous qualities recorded which distinguish the Christian from the non-Christian. For example, the apostle Peter wrote "because Christ suffered for you, leaving you an example, . . . you should follow in his steps" (1 Pet. 2:21, NIV). Peter also raised the most basic question possible about the Christian pattern of life when he asked: "What manner of persons ought ye to be?" (2 Pet. 3:11). There are at least three major characteristics of the Christian life-style which are magnified in Bible teaching.

First, the Christian life-style is a *positive* way of living. The Christian life is one that glorifies Christ because it is the product of the Holy Spirit. Paul described this kind of life with words like "love, joy, peace, patience, kindness, goodness, faithfulness, gentleness, self-control" (Gal. 5:22, Williams).

Second, the Christian life-style is a *disciplined* way of living. The natural desires and cravings of man's own way of life are the exact opposite of the spiritual nature. These two natures constantly oppose each other and thereby create conflicting ways of life. For example, it is natural to be jealous, angry, and divisive; but it is Christian to be trusting, peaceful, and conciliatory. It is natural to engage in carnal acts such as drunkenness and immorality; but it is Christian to avoid revelry, drunkenness, and unchastity.

Third, the Christian life-style is a *balanced* way of living. The word *balanced* does not refer to an equality of good and bad behavior. Rather, it refers to the balance between what is believed and what is practiced. It also refers to a balance between faith and works, between devotion and effective service to God. Again, the word *balanced* refers to a balance between the intellectual response and the emotional response to God. It refers to the difference between what is and what ought to be. And finally, the word speaks to the matter of balance between Christian ministry and Christian witnessing. James, the beloved pastor of the church at Jerusalem, spoke poignantly to the matter of balance in the Christian life when he asked: "My brothers, what good is there in a man's saying that he has faith, if he has no good deeds to prove it?" (Jas. 2:14, Williams).

6. Bible Teaching Cultivates a Christlike Personality

Personality is all too often viewed primarily as the impression one makes on another person, with special emphasis on the energy level that is displayed. Personality is far more than this limited view. Human personality is the combination of an individual's characteristics. It includes the physical structure, the pattern of thinking, the manner of perception, the pattern of response, the style of behavior, and even the tone of voice.

Because all persons have some measure of these essential characteristics, all persons have personality. Even those individuals who make no perceptible impression, contribute nothing of themselves to others, and are distressingly bland cannot be considered as having no personality. Even these persons emit a form of personality although it may be considered as a positively negative form!

The Bible has a great influence on personality and so does teaching. But teachers need to respect the divine provision of individuality. God does not intend that everyone be alike. It is a mistake to pressure or even overly persuade anyone, to imitate another person. The only perfect model is Jesus Christ. Redeemed persons are designed to be like him, but it is only realistic to recognize that perfection of that kind is unattainable by man. Even though man bears the image of God and possesses the component parts of the divine personality, the goal of complete Christlikeness is never reached in the present world. On the other hand, even though certain boundaries are set by heredity, every personality can be modified to a remarkable degree. And it is particularly true that the person who has been saved enjoys a whole new potential for improvement. This new potential manifests itself in three ways:

First, in the new birth the Christian receives a new mind. The Christian mind is not just refashioned or made over. It is made anew. There is an entirely new potential for "wisdom, and righteousness, and sanctification, and redemption." (See 1 Cor. 1:30.)

Second, the Christian has a new capacity for love. This new faculty is not just an enlarged capacity. It is a completely new ability. It is the capacity to love God and the ability to love other persons in the way God loves. John put it this way: "Beloved, let us love one another: for love is of God; and every one that loveth is born of God, and knoweth God" (1 John 4:7).

Third, when a person becomes a Christian, one receives a new volitional power. It is the capacity to determine the will of God, the commitment to do the will of God, and the ability to will to do God's will. Even though this new capacity is inherent in the new birth, it is the most difficult of all of the personality components to change. Mankind's self-willfulness was the essential cause of the disaster that overtook man in the fall. The will is also the last stronghold of the natural man against the spiritual man. When the Christian comes to the place of handing over one's own will to the will of God, one will have blessed fellowship between his or her mind and God's mind, between his or her heart and God's heart, and between his or her will and God's will. On reaching this state of Christian development, the believer has grown into a personality that is wholesome, healthy, and Christlike.

It is not likely that Bible teaching should focus primarily on changing and improving personality. If growth of the learner is the basic goal—and it is—then personality improvement is a concomitant of learning. And when personality improvement does occur, it is a valid evidence that teaching has been successful and learning has been authentic.

7. Bible Teaching Produces a Sense of Responsibility

Two great concerns must come to dominate the heart and life of the Christian. One is the multiplied millions of unredeemed persons and the other is a growing sense of personal responsibility for these persons.

In a day when irresponsibility is so prevalent that phrases like "cop out" are invented to describe the condition, it seems that Christians are also tending to be less responsive to the lost and less responsible in witnessing to them. Why? Perhaps the meaning of responsibility is misunderstood and the characteristics of a responsible person are not clear.

A responsible person is one who has the capacity to see what needs to be done, the ability to devise a way to do it, and the determination to do it as effectively as possible. From this definitive statement four characteristics of a responsible person emerge. (1) A responsible person has enough self-confidence to believe that he can do what is required by the circumstance; (2) a responsible person has enough creativeness to help him perceive the way to meet the challenge; (3) a responsible person has a kind of courage that enables him to face the challenge; and (4) the responsible person has a spirit of decisiveness which keeps him at the task until it is completed.

These qualities are generally associated with certain types of personality, yet they seem to be more evident in the life of a growing Christian. It is difficult to avoid the conclusion that a morally responsible person is much more likely to respond to a challenge, especially if the challenge is in the best interest of all persons concerned. Christianity adds a new dimension to the concept of responsibility.

In the struggle to become mature and responsible Christians, it seems significant that Bible study is the major contributing factor to this kind of growth. This causal effect not only makes the Sunday School a vital factor in developing responsible Christians, but it also magnifies the role of the Sunday School in building a sense of responsibility for the unsaved masses. Among the many ways in which the Sunday School through its Bible teaching activities develops a sense of responsibility for the lost, are these:

1. Interprets the meaning of lostness;
2. Teaches the way to salvation;
3. Reinforces compassion for persons;
4. Stimulates participation in outreach;
5. Includes training in witness;
6. Undergirds evangelistic activities;
7. Brings unsaved persons into the worship services;
8. Fosters personal ministries which lead to evangelism;
9. Instills the proper motivations for outreach and evangelism;
10. Provides prayer support for cultivation and witnessing.

8. Bible Teaching Creates Church Growth

Although it is true that a few churches seem to grow with little or no Sunday School provision, it is not true that churches grow without some kind of Bible teaching activities. In many ways Bible teaching is the most critical factor in church growth. Consider the cataclysmic consequences if there were no Bible, if a church laid aside the Bible, or if a teacher ignored the Bible or taught it poorly. What would the result be? The church would have no message. The church would know nothing about its mandate. The church would have no definitive mission. The church would have no workable program or methodology. The church would be devoid of any motivation. Because of the Bible teaching responsibility of the Sunday School, the church which has no Sunday School, or has a very weak and ineffective one, has no indisputable opportunity to be what a church is alleged to be.

There is no way to avoid the conclusion that the early New Testament churches made much of the teaching of the Holy Scriptures. To be sure, they had to rely on the teaching of the apostles as well, but the material taught by the apostles is now a part of the New Testament. Bible teaching then, as now, is inherently required in authentic church growth. This outcome is why teaching was then, and is now, a sacred priority.

Bible teaching produces the potential for church growth. This Bible study and Bible teaching are the secret to reaching people. Although many things are involved in the motivation to attend Sunday School, the final and ultimate decision is based on the quality of the Bible study situation. People are interested in Bible study because it deals with the major issues of life, death, and the hereafter. Bible study is intellectually stimulating, socially rewarding, personally satisfying, and psychologically fulfilling. In addition, these matters together create an atmosphere that is spiritually uplifting. These facts mean that the Bible has a drawing power that is never blunted by time or familiarity with the Scriptures. Because of these special attractions in Bible study, churches need to keep their Sunday School conscious of the fact that their role in reaching out to people is immensely important to the church.

Bible teaching also develops a concern for growth. This fact accounts for the overarching concern for outreach which has always characterized the Sunday School that has quality teaching. This concern is not for numbers but for persons. The concern may be expressed in quantitative terms, but the expression is only a promotional handle for reaching persons. Numerical growth is simply an easy way to measure response to Christ's concern for people and to acknowledge the fact that a church is responsible for reaching people for Bible study, Christ, and church membership. It is ludicrous to think that Christians would give themselves to the time and effort required to reach numbers of people if their only motivation is a "craze for numbers."

Bible teaching and its concomitant, Bible study, are both essential to the authenticity of a church. Bible teaching is also vital to the spiritual growth of Christians. In childhood, Bible teaching is foundational. In youth, Bible teaching is stabilizing. In adulthood, Bible study is supportive and assuring. Therefore, for the church and for persons of all ages, Bible study has the potential for being the most valuable and productive of all church efforts. Furthermore, Bible teaching makes the largest single contribution to the growth of the church. Given these two dynamic potentials, Bible teaching should be given the foremost position and the utmost consideration of all church activities. When such priority is given and the Bible is properly taught, the result will be both corporate and personal benefits beyond any conceivable measure.

As the body of Christ, a church has several important functions. Foremost among these is Bible teaching and the inherent disposition to reach out to involve persons in Bible study which this function generates. In the twentieth century the Sunday School has become the church's organization for planning, conducting, and evaluating its Bible teaching ministry. The Sunday School, because of what it has been, what it now is, and what it can become is the best vehicle available to generate and assimilate church growth. Any present skepticism or any uneasiness about the future of the Sunday School will vanish rapidly if careful consideration is given to what the Sunday School is already doing for the church. Its supreme significance is seen in the following statements:

1. If a church did not have a Sunday School it would have no systematic approach to teaching the Word of God to persons of all ages.

2. If a church did not have a Sunday School, it would have no way to administer an organized effort to reach persons who are outside the influence of the church.

3. If a church had no Sunday School, it would have no continuing opportunity to use the gifts and talents of a significant number of its members.

4. If a church had no Sunday School, there would be no formalized plan for influencing church members and prospects.

5. If a church had no Sunday School, it would be unable to make any serious attempt to involve large numbers of people in Christian worship.

6. If a church had no Sunday School, it would have no effective avenue for presenting a continuous witness to lost persons.

7. If a church had no Sunday School, it would have no consistent way to instruct and enlist its members in stewardship.

8. If a church had no Sunday School, it would be without any specific process for providing Christian nurture and growth for its children and youth.

9. If a church had no Sunday School, it would have no life-long means for helping adults mature in their spiritual and emotional life.

10. If a church had no Sunday School, it would have no viable alternative to falling back on less effective approaches or creating a new organization that would do the very same things the Sunday School is already providing.

8

Evangelizing the Lost
for Growth

The popular concept of evangelism is limited in its scope. Evangelism, as popularly conceived, is simply the phenomenon of conversion or being born again. This second birth is certainly the central focus in evangelism. Yet in the thinking of many people, conversion is synonymous with Christ's command to *make disciples*. Biblically, however, conversion is only one aspect of making disciples. Such confusion requires clarification.

The English word *evangelism* is simply a general concept word. It is not even found in the Bible. However, a number of more specific terms do occur. The Greek word *euaggelion* means good news or glad tidings. It refers to the *content* of the gospel message. The Greek word *euaggelizo* means to announce, to proclaim good news. It refers to the *proclamation* of the gospel by teaching and preaching. The Greek word *euaggelistes* means to give witness to the power of the gospel. It refers to the *person* in the role of evangelist. These three concepts speak to the *content* of the gospel, the *spread* of the gospel, and the *authentication* of the gospel. However, the full meaning of evangelism cannot be understood apart from a comprehension of the total scope of *salvation*.

The Bible pictures salvation (*soteria*) from three different but significantly related perspectives: First, salvation is an *instantaneous experience* which is regeneration, the new birth. Second, salvation is a *continuing process* which is sanctification, growth in discipleship. Third, salvation is an *ultimate state* which is glorification, eternity in the presence of Christ.

Does the Sunday School have any part to play in these immensely important matters? Indeed it does! Not just because it is a Sunday School, not just because it is the foremost organization in a church, not just because it is a part of the most significant movement in Christianity. How then is the Sunday School related to the evangelistic mission of the church?

The Sunday School's role in evangelism grows out of its *nature* as the church's structure for reaching people. Its role emerges from its innate *functions* in finding, cultivating, teaching, and witnessing to, lost persons. Its role is inherent in its *utility* in channeling the evangelistic gifts of its members. In every conceivable way the Sunday School is uniquely suited to providing the evangelistic thrust in church growth.

If these roles in evangelism are valid—and all empirical evidence indicates that they are—then the Sunday School is a church's most *positive* and most *potent* force in evangelism. By using the Sunday School to the extent of its potential, any church can reap a far greater evangelistic harvest than it could do otherwise. And by failing to use its Sunday School appropriately, any church is failing to capitalize on its most "thrust-worthy" ally in evangelism. Here are some very practical means a church can use to develop a Sunday School evangelistic thrust.

1. Use the Sunday School to Create an Evangelistic Atmosphere

Most Christians understand that personal witnessing is every Christian's job, and that evangelism is every church's occupation. They also know that most Christians do not reach this grand ideal and that few churches realize their evangelistic potential. This failure is sometimes caused by willful disobedience, more often by self-centered considerations, and most generally by simple neglect. However, all failure grows out of an atmosphere that does not stimulate or motivate witnessing and evangelism. It is at this point of creating a wholesome evangelistic atmosphere that the Sunday School can be especially helpful.

(1) Affirm the Reality of Lostness

The early Christians were convinced that "lostness" was not confined to the pagans around them. These Christians understood that even the sincere practitioners of traditional religion were also lost unless they had personally received the gift of God's grace. They knew that lost persons had a tragic sin problem and that they faced a terrible plight because of sin. They taught these truths fearlessly, and they preached Christ as the only hope for salvation.

Everyone who works in the Sunday School needs to be certain about the reality of sin and its consequences. Without this certainty it is impossible to affirm faithfully the tragic truth about sin and its traumatic outcome. The Sunday School must communicate the fact that sinners are lost and desperately need to be saved. Sunday School leaders and members need to realize afresh that to tone down or ignore the plight of unsaved persons will inevitably lead to a soft or negligent attitude toward witnessing, a cooling of the evangelistic atmosphere, and a gradual decline in the outreach and growth of the church.

(2) Stimulate Concern for Unsaved Persons

Most Christians would readily agree that making disciples is the basic assignment of a church, and most have at least a vague feeling of oughtness about personal witnessing. Nevertheless, few Christians actually witness on a continuing basis. Why is this the case? Probably it stems from the fact that most Christians do not have enough personal contact with unsaved individuals to experience any empathetic emotion, much less any genuine compassion.

Compassion and *concern* are difficult words to define in the

Christian context. These emotions are even more difficult to experience. The difficulty is that they are divine emotions which are unidirectional. Human emotions are usually reciprocal. They are generated by interacting personalities. They are bidirectional in nature. It is difficult to feel or express a spiritual concern for a mere acquaintance, much less for an unknown person or for a person who is actually disliked. Herein lies the difficulty in feeling concern or expressing compassion for most unsaved persons. Because they are unknown, there is little opportunity to develop a compassionate concern for them until they become personally known and individually understood in the light of their unique need.

Apparently the first step in developing concern is to become involved in the process of discovering and coming to know lost persons. Therefore, church leaders need to plan Sunday School activities that will impel workers and members to make deliberate efforts to search for, identify, and cultivate unsaved individuals. Fortunately, the Sunday School has a large number of search/discovery plans and projects described in numerous books and program helps.

Experience verifies the fact that any kind of search activity is a magnificent means for developing and deepening concern for persons. It could well be that people-searching-for-people projects are as important in developing concern as they are for finding and reaching people. The Scriptures indicate that seeing the people in their needs resulted in Jesus' feeling deep compassion for them (Matt. 9:36). Thus it appears that proximity to the prospects was a stimulus to compassion even for Jesus, the most concerned person of all time!

(3) Keep the Evangelistic Motive Central

Of all the church activities, the ones related to outreach, witnessing, evangelism, and missions have the most widespread range of motivations. Many activities carry an evangelistic label when in reality they are primarily planned to fulfill the desire of leaders and members to "go places and do things." Therefore, it is quite appropriate to ponder this question: "Are we really doing these things out of an evangelistic motivation?"

The problem of motivation is by no means confined to Sunday School workers. Serving in the energy of the flesh is a human weakness visible in the highest pulpit to the lowest pew. It is not unknown even among the "super saints"—persons who claim to have the *gift of evangelism* and who glory in it as if it were limited only to themselves when, in reality, every Christian has some evangelistic contribution to make.

At this point it needs to be emphasized that *any* approach to evangelism that excludes the Sunday School or ignores its potential is exceedingly shortsighted. Furthermore, such plans are all but doomed to failure at the outset because they bypass or minimize a veritable army of Christian workers—persons who are already paying the church's price for evangelism by their discovering, cultivating, teaching, and ministry efforts. To be shunted aside from their evangelistic contributions only makes their own witnessing more difficult and less fruitful. In addition to being evangelistically rejected, the age-group expertise of these people is immediately lost to any evangelistic strategy. Evangelistic motivations must not only be generated; they must also be preserved.

2. Use the Sunday School to Enroll Non-Christians

When the full concept of salvation and the proper understanding of evangelism are taken into account, there can be no doubt about the need for Bible teaching in the making of disciples. It is in this frame of reference that enrollment in Sunday School finds its significance. Willingness to become enrolled in Bible study may seem to a long-time Christian like a small matter, but to an unsaved person it is often a frightening and difficult step.

Sunday School enrollment begins a mutual acceptance of the

responsibilities involved in Bible teaching and Bible study. It is the initial step in a relationship that has *eternal implications.* Enrollment is a matter of great consequence because it begins a spiritual chain of cause and effect. It frequently closes the gates of hell and opens the doors of heaven!

Before it makes any responsible effort to enroll non-Christians, a Sunday School must settle the matter of membership requirements. The most effective way to keep unsaved persons out of Bible study is to set up membership criteria. This insidious malpractice has plagued many Sunday Schools for years. It is the unchristian practice of requiring new people to meet some test of serious intent before they are allowed to enroll. This unwholesome attitude is generally expressed by requiring prospective members to complete a three-Sunday attendance record before they are accepted as members. Such a requirement is illogical, inconsiderate, and discriminatory. Most of the present members of any given class could not pass such a requirement! Membership requirements make a Sunday School seem like a club, a lodge, or some other fraternal order. *The Sunday School should be the easiest thing in the world to join, and the most difficult thing in the world to "de-join!"*

Non-Christians, like everyone else, should not only be welcome to join the Sunday School immediately; they should be expeditiously urged to do so. As a matter of fact, most unsaved persons should *already be members of the Sunday School before they attend.* They should be preenrolled in the home, with their permission, of course. In this way they can be welcomed on Sunday as a *new member.* Is it not true that no one needs the Sunday School more than an unsaved person? And is it not true also that the Sunday School needs to reach the unsaved person more than anyone else? From every conceivable perspective it seems that Sunday School membership should be open to anyone, at any time, at any church. This would be the case if every Sunday School had a sign on its "heart" with these words: *Compassion at work here.*

Sunday Schools generally have difficulty enrolling non-Christians simply because their organization is inadequate or inappropriate. In addition to having too few teaching units, particularly in the adult division, most of the present units are saturated. Saturation does not mean necessarily that the meeting place is full. It does mean that the organization is "full" because it is doing all that the teacher and class are capable of doing, or are willing to do to reach lost people.

A great deal of the evangelistic stalemate in most churches is the inevitable result of failure to create more teaching units, especially in the adult division. A study of the high point in evangelism in any church almost always shows that the most people are brought to Christ soon after the creation of new adult teaching units. There is an incredible correlation, if not a causal connection, between the creation of new adult units and an upsurge in evangelism.

In addition to new units, there are several other organizational adjustments which produce a positive effect on evangelism. For example, (1) realigning the organizational units with the current population trends in the community; (2) strengthening the visitation program of the Sunday School; (3) updating the grading and promotion procedures; (4) upgrading the quality of teaching and learning activities; (5) improving the leadership selection and deployment process; (6) developing a continuing plan of leadership training; (7) enhancing the attractiveness of space and equipment; (8) reassigning space to provide more room for growth; (9) introducing new enrollment procedures; (10) providing personal assistance to new members and visitors in locating appropriate units.

In many areas a special inquirers' class is not only possible but highly desirable. This provision is especially suited to rapidly growing population centers. Such a class would require a highly competent teacher(s) but no organization, membership, or attendance requirements. The purpose would be to help persons understand who a Christian is and what a Christian should be like. The obvious goal of such an unusual class is evangelism.

3. Use the Sunday School to Develop Relationships with the Lost

Because people are social beings, harmonious and supportive relationships are essential. This desire for social contact, friendship, and companionship varies from person to person, but everyone possesses the drive and seeks to satisfy the desire.

Although fellowship sometimes overrides the generation gap, most fellowship is a peer-group experience. Because the Sunday School is a peer-group organization, it has a unique opportunity to relate persons of similar needs, interests, and outlooks. The very nature of the Sunday School organization makes it ideally suited to developing a wholesome and meaningful relationship with non-Christians. All regular sessions, social occasions, fellowship activities, visitation experiences, and get-acquainted projects should include prospective members, especially the non-Christians who are being cultivated. These persons feel keenly about being included. To be left out is like being shut out. To be overlooked is to feel unwanted. To be ignored is to feel rejected.

The Sunday School is an ideal instrument in developing a caring relationship with the lost. The early Christian churches were aware of the needs of people that stood in the way of their need for Christ. They fed the hungry, healed the sick, helped the fallen, encouraged the weak, comforted the sorrowing, resolved the differences, shared their possessions, and rejoiced in their fellowship. In all of their sharing, caring was evident. These Christlike activities developed beautiful relationships with non-Christians for it is recorded that they enjoyed "favour with all the people. And the Lord added to the church daily such as should be saved" (Acts 2:47).

4. Use the Sunday School to Interpret the Gospel

Bible teaching looms large in every approach to evangelism. It played a highly significant role in the evangelistic work of the early churches. Although those original churches did not have the New Testament, they used the Old Testament Scriptures to proclaim the good news, to interpret the life of Christ, to explain the redemptive work of Christ, and to convince the lost they needed Christ. Furthermore, they used the Scriptures to instruct new converts.

Bible teaching is also the crux of the evangelistic work of the Sunday School. These observations are not intended to mean that Bible teaching, or even Bible knowledge in itself, saves an individual. They do indicate that Bible teaching plays a major role in bringing people to Christ. There is ample evidence that both Bible teaching and Bible study produce conviction for sin and a realization of the need for salvation. In New Testament evangelism, Bible teaching both preceded and followed the conversion experience. The apostle Paul gave the reason for this procedure: "For it is the power of God unto salvation to every one that believeth" (Rom. 1:16*b*). The writer of Hebrews explained what the Bible does: "For the word of God is living and active, sharper than any two-edged sword, piercing to the division of soul and spirit, of joints and marrow, and discerning the thoughts and intentions of the heart" (4:12, RSV).

The Bible teaching hour of the Sunday School is the ideal situation for interpreting the gospel both for the saved and the unsaved. In this setting the Sunday School is finely focused on its preeminent priority. This teaching-learning experience is the genius of the Sunday School, the heartbeat of Christianity. An evangelistic appeal every Sunday is neither needed or desirable. However, under the appropriate circumstances it is not only desirable; it is imperative. Presenting the "plan of salvation" each week is illogical and redundant, but when it comes naturally from the Scriptures being studied, it is both logical and desirable. Because the Sunday School is preeminently compatible to teaching the Bible to non-Christians; and, because the Bible is from first to last a redemptive resource; and, because the Holy Spirit works through the Scriptures to bring persons to salvation, it is imperative that Bible teaching sound an evangelistic note and interpret the message and meaning of the gospel.

5. Use the Sunday School to Do Evangelistic Visitation

Both the amazing evangelistic thrust and the unparalleled growth of the Jerusalem church were the direct result of evangelistic visitation. Luke described this visitation vividly: "*And daily* in the temple, and in *every* house, they *ceased not* to *teach* and *preach Jesus Christ*" (Acts 5:42, author's italics). These few words reveal a great deal about the visitation program of that first church. Their evangelistic visitation was (1) *continuous* because it was in operation every day; (2) *conspicuous* because it began in the Temple; (3) *comprehensive* because it included every house; (4) *consistent* because "they ceased not to teach and preach"; (5) *credible* because the message was Jesus Christ; (6) *compassionate* because nothing else would motivate such an unprecedented approach to evangelism.

Just as Christ's mission was "to seek and to save that which was lost" (Luke 19:10), so is the church's mission to *seek* and to *find* lost persons. Stated in a more theological form, *the mission of a church is to bring persons to God through Jesus Christ*. This mission requires a church to engage constantly and conscientiously in *evangelistic* visitation. And *the Sunday School is the way in which a church structures itself to accomplish this unique mission*.

The key to an evangelistic church is not a select group of evangelism experts. That approach is far too limited. *The real key is to mobilize and field every member possible in continuous, concentrated, consistent, Christ-centered, and compassionate visitation of its basic community*.

There is no magic formula, no secret set of growth principles, no superproductive style of leadership, no guaranteed-to-work methods, and no exclusive or inclusive doctrinal statement that will automatically produce lasting church growth. Growth occurs *now* like it always *has*. It is the result of a divine *message*, delivered by a motivated *messenger*, using a biblical *method*. The divine *message* is "Christ died to save sinners." The *motivation* is "the love of Christ." The *method* is "Go ye" from person to person. This Sunday School oriented approach to evangelism will revolutionize everything a church does, especially in the area of corporate evangelism. It will get evangelism done in the *right place*—out of the church building into the lost world. It will get evangelism done in the *right way*—a personal sharing of the gospel rather than Christians giving testimonies to each other. It will get evangelism beamed to the *right people*— the unsaved masses rather than the "faithful few." It will get evangelism centered on the *right thing*—the reality of the new birth rather than the frailty of a commendable life-style. It will get evangelism directed to the *right generation*—the millions of unsaved adults rather than the children of the members who are frequently too young to know they are lost.

6. Use the Sunday School to Assure "Everywhere" Witnessing

It is said of the early Christians that they "went everywhere preaching the Good News about Jesus" (Acts 8:4, TLB). The self-evident inference is that they took advantage of each witness opportunity and even created opportunities to share the good news.

This "everywhere" evangelism concept is the pivotal method in the Great Commission. Every Christian should learn to be alert to obvious evangelistic opportunities. Every Sunday School worker should be sensitive to situations which could be developed into witnessing opportunities. Every individual Christian, every church member should take advantage of those fleeting once-in-a-lifetime opportunities.

An even more important aspect of "everywhere" evangelism is the willingness to take advantage of those special times for witnessing in the daily contacts with people. There are many events and situations in life that create a favorable opportunity to share a personal word of witness or to evidence a vital faith. All interpersonal relationships are ready-made opportunities to share Christ.

"Everywhere" evangelism is appropriate at home, on the job, at school, in the office, at the store, in the shop, or in the marketplace. Social contacts appropriate for a Christian should be used for witnessing purposes. Special events such as sports, hobbies, clubs, organizations, and civic affairs may serve as witnessing outlets.

The "everywhere" approach makes every Christian not only a witness for Christ but a missionary as well. The "everywhere" of each Christian is different and is his own unique world of opportunity. Moreover, the method of "everywhere" evangelism is just as personal as the opportunity is unique. Each can use the approach that fits one's own personality, thought patterns, vocabulary, and temperament. Each can adapt one's witnessing style to the occasion and the situation. There is no need for a stereotyped approach and no reason to try to imitate some other person. There is really no need for a memorized plan, a set of props, or a "sure-fire" answer for every question or problem encountered. Witnessing is communication. It is a normal conversation. It is an exchange of personal thoughts and commitments about the reality of one's faith in Jesus Christ.

Jesus witnessed to the woman of Samaria through a simple conversation about water. The immoral woman who had had five husbands found Christ and brought her friends to someone who could help. Philip discussed the meaning of a passage of Scripture. Paul shared his personal experience and used it as an opportunity to persuade others. Each one of these very different approaches is valid as is any other that gets to the point of presenting Christ.

The simplicity of the gospel and the meaning of evangelism are often obscured by the many words, concepts, and approaches used in the Bible and in church life. The methods of communication are: (1) *teaching*—explaining the gospel; (2) *witnessing*—sharing the gospel; (3) *evangelizing*—spreading the gospel; and (4) *preaching*—proclaiming the gospel. All four methods can be done professionally, but *none* of them has to be. No *one* of the methods is better than any other. No *one* of them has to be used exclusively. They may all be used individually, separately, collectively, or interchangeably. Methodology in "everywhere" evangelism is relatively unimportant. The important thing is using the opportunity. Success is not required. Not everyone responded to Jesus. The Christian's responsibility is to communicate Christ. The Holy Spirit is responsible for conviction. The unsaved individual is accountable for his own response.

The facts of the gospel are beautifully simple. In essence there are only two: (1) persons are lost; (2) Jesus saves. These facts are portrayed in numerous places in the New Testament, and they may be readily learned, even memorized. However, a person who witnesses does not have to know everything about the Bible. Witnessing is simply *introducing a person to Christ*. Sharing one's own testimony in the process may or may not be required. Witnessing is a person-to-person act. It may be difficult and slow, but it is the very essence of New Testament evangelism.[1]

1. Portions of this chapter are abstracted from John T. Sisemore, *Witness to Win* (Nashville: Convention Press, 1978), chapter 3. All rights reserved. Used by permission.

9

Assimilating New Members For Growth

The spectrum of church growth is generally viewed simply as a matter of bringing persons to Christ and into church membership. To be sure, both of these important matters are included in church growth. However, that concept is far too simplistic to cover the full range of operations involved in authentic church growth. Any valid concept of the church growth process must include a wider classification of the several outreach activities and inclusive relationships that are involved. The following listing, though not exhaustive, is comprehensive enough to illustrate the vast scope of the growth process:

1. Discovering prospective members;
2. Developing relationships with the prospective members;
3. Helping prospects feel wanted and accepted;
4. Involving responsive persons in church organizations;
5. Evangelizing unsaved persons;
6. Bringing new Christians into church membership;
7. Orienting new adherents to the local congregation;
8. Involving new members in the outreach activities;
9. Inducting qualified persons into leadership roles;
10. Assimilating all members into the life and work of the church family.

Although the various growth operations have been listed in a chronological order they do not necessarily occur in such a neat sequence, or in any special order for that matter. Several aspects of the growth process may operate at or near the same time, some of the steps may not occur at all at a given time, and some of the operations will never be needed for some people. Furthermore, in some cases the sequences may appear to be illogical, but it should be remembered that spiritual matters do not necessarily operate according to natural order. Nevertheless, each one of the operations is essential if there is to be a healthy and lasting growth pattern in a church.

Most churches and church leaders would accept this total process concept as a valid principle but they would tacitly reject it in actual practice. For example, a feeling of inclusion is especially difficult for some people to achieve, especially if they are not long-time residents or well-known persons in the community. Numerous persons are to be found in the membership of every church who seem to feel excluded, or at least do not feel included in the more meaningful aspects of church life. To be bluntly truthful about the matter, most churches practice some form of exclusionary tactics. Many members who do feel included do not realize this problem. In fact it would be difficult to convince them that it is true. However, it is a prevalent problem. The evidence of the exclusionary bias is seen in the way some persons react to the church in which they hold membership. For instance, in most churches, about one half of the total membership has just faded away. These members are dropouts. They rarely, if ever, attend. They contribute little, if any at all. They do not participate in any church activity. They are generally critical of the church. And many resent and even resist any effort to restore them to participative fellowship. In reality these persons are a living negation of almost everything a church is trying to achieve.

Second, there are numerous former members of churches who have silently slipped away and united with a "sister church" in the same area. These individuals almost always feel rejected. They have sought acceptance in another church.

Third, there are in most churches recently accepted new

members who showed promise of developing into stable and useful members, yet they soon become irregular, indifferent, and often completely inactive. These persons are demonstrating their feeling that although they were accepted into the church *membership*, they were not accepted into the *fellowship*.

Fourth, there are other people who recently moved into the community, visited the church one or more times, but eventually discovered that they were not right for the church so they decided not to become involved.

Although these four groups of persons expressed their feelings of dissatisfaction in somewhat different ways, none of them felt included. They either experienced or believed that they experienced some form of exclusion, if not actual rejection. Their lack of satisfaction, and eventual disassociation, indicated that they preferred nonassociation to exclusion. Admittedly, there may have been other factors which caused the feeling of rejection. These persons may have misunderstood the situation or even created their own problem. Yet they did not feel accepted, nor did they find the sense of belonging that they needed. On the other hand, it is quite generally understood that people go where they feel wanted, remain where they feel accepted, and absent themselves when they feel unwelcome. Regardless of the exact nature of the problems involved, or the identity of the persons at fault, these unhappy experiences are prima facie evidence of a break down in the assimilation of new members.

Because the successful assimilation of new people is the final test of a church's ability to grow, and because assimilation is an acquired church skill, it is extremely important for a church to understand the process and be able to manage its assimilation operation. And then, too, because the Sunday School has the greatest potential for creating, enhancing, and preserving the relationship between a church and its members, it is essential that a church capitalize on this magnificent endowment. Although the Sunday School can make a significant contribution to the total process of church growth, there are several specific ways in which it excels in the incorporation and assimilation of new members into the organized life and work of the church.

1. The Sunday School Produces a Feeling of Acceptance

Next to having the basic provisions for survival, human beings desire personal acceptance above almost everything else. In some ways this desire is so strong that it may appear to be an evidence of insecurity, but it is much more an innate need for a sense of community. This need is magnified by a culture that stresses togetherness, gentleness, and tenderness. When these things are lacking the roots of loneliness are very deep, so much so that even the slightest sarcasm, flippant manner, or pointed silence may intensify one's feelings of aloneness. Chronic aloneness has become a universal source of psychic suffering. It contributes to all of the ills of persons and society in general. When aloneness is caused by feelings of exclusion or is accompanied by a sense of personal unworthiness, the damage is all-pervasive.

Although the Sunday School is by no means a psychological recovery room, it offers the beneficial form of acceptance and feelings of personal worth. It has no peer in providing a wholesome atmosphere of being welcome, wanted, and needed. These values grow out of the fact that a Sunday School can induct its new members in a cordial and compassionate manner.

If a Sunday School is to do its best job in assimilating new members it must begin with improving its approach to receiving and inducting new members. The following plan is both practical and effective. It is presented on the adult level, but it may be readily adapted to any age level.

(1) Procedure for the Department Leadership

- Extend publicly a warm and personal welcome on the Sunday a new member joins the Sunday School. Relate some of the interesting facts about the person's home, employment, family, and background.

- Present some memento such as a New Testament as a reminder of the new relationship to the department.
- Make sure that the new member is appropriately presented to the teacher and other class leaders.
- Mention to the new member some of the opportunities for personal involvement in the department.
- According to the interest and qualification of the new member, involve him in some aspect of the department work as soon as possible.

(2) *Procedure for the Class Leadership*

- Introduce the new member to the class members and help him feel welcome and accepted.
- Assign the new member to a group, and have the group leader escort the member through the session and to the worship service.
- Provide a member's study periodical and a Bible if the member did not bring one.
- Make sure that the members take a personal interest in the new member and ask them to give a guided tour of the church facilities.

(3) *Procedure for Follow-Up During the Week*

- Have the teacher and group leader visit the new member as soon as possible to develop a personal friendship.
- Explain the use of the periodical, and show the member how to prepare for the class session.
- Interpret the record system, time schedule, parking provisions, and locations of places for other family members and friends.
- Check on other family members, relatives, and friends who may be prospective members.
- Encourage regular attendance and immediate involvement.

- Discover the new member's interest and apprehensions about participation in the study session.
- Assure the new member of your genuine concern for his spiritual growth and your desire for him to become a part of the spiritual fellowship of the class.

(4) Procedure for Subsequent Visits

- Pray with and for the new member.
- Seek to involve the member in the outreach and ministry activities of the class as appropriate.
- Enlist the member for attendance at the class meetings and social activities.
- Contact the member to encourage participation in any areas of noninvolvement, and affirm his participation in the things he does.
- Enlist the new member in any plan for new member orientation and interpret the procedures.
- Accompany the member to special church events and fellowship activities.

2. The Sunday School Produces a Sense of Belonging

Closely akin to a feeling of acceptance is a sense of belonging. Acceptance may be defined as a state of being included while belonging is a state of being closely associated. The difference between the two states is one of degree more than one of kind. As a rule, a sense of belonging grows out of a feeling of acceptance, and a feeling of acceptance emerges from one's own level of self-esteem. In other words, a feeling of acceptance is largely personal and a sense of belonging is primarily an interpersonal matter.

These psychological dynamics may seem unimportant to an individual who already enjoys a strong sense of belonging. However, acceptance and belonging are so important to prospective members, especially unsaved persons, that little else matters to them in so far as church life is concerned. As a matter of fact, any effort to assimilate new members must recognize and work in harmony with this universal need to belong. This need to belong was recently illustrated when the author asked a prospective church member where his membership was. He replied: "I'm a member of _____ Church but I don't really belong anywhere." Quite obviously, belonging should be synonymous with membership but it isn't always that way.

As the outreach arm of the church, the Sunday School should develop an expertise in helping persons come to a wholesome sense of belonging. This endeavor should be based on the proposition that *recruitment for membership involves a total acceptance of the new member and an unrelenting effort to help the member experience a deep sense of belonging.* Failure to do so is at least hypocritical if not a negation of the spirit of Christ. Recruiting without accepting is the major cause of the huge backlog of disappointed and disillusioned members of both the Sunday School and church. Moreover, the cliquishness of those who have a strong sense of belonging is probably a major reason for the lack of growth and the disaffection of members which are being experienced by some churches.

Producing a sense of belonging is an ongoing challenge which requires numerous approaches but only a modicum of time. The broad spectrum of possible activities may be illustrated under three headings.

(1) Value persons as divine originals.

In spite of the many efforts to characterize and classify persons, no two individuals are alike, or can be alike. Each person is a unique individual—a divine original. And because God does not want any of his creatures to perish, it is essential that Christians learn to accept, appreciate, and identify with every prospective Christian and church member. Because spiritual potential is sometimes disguised as human impotence, it is important that persons be valued for what they are as well as for what they may become.

(2) Affirm individuals as significant persons.

Unfortunately many church people see the unsaved, unreached, unconcerned person primarily as a prospective opportunity to increase the numerical and financial strength of the church. They do not fully recognize uninvolved persons for what they really are—opportunities for God's grace to do its work. To be sure, the persons may be unresponsive, even unlovable, and undesirable as friends, yet they are significant in God's sight. They are potential jewels for his crown.

Sunday School leaders and members alike can affirm persons for what they are without having to approve what they are not. Affirmation activities should always be based on specific, wholesome, and positive things which a person has done. Any affirming activity must be done wtih integrity and without any ulterior motivation. The genuine affirmation of persons is a basic step in assimilating individuals into the membership and fellowship of the Sunday School and church.

(3) Reinforce positive responses.

Helping persons develop a sense of belonging requires careful and sensitive follow-through. Each time an individual makes a positive step he should be reinforced and strengthened by an activity which has meaning and relevance to him. These follow-through activities may take any number of forms. In fact, the type of activity is likely less important than the fact that a sincere effort was made to recognize and approve the response. Reinforcement activities may include a simple word of appreciation, an assurance of prayer about a personal concern of the individual, an inquiry about a matter that holds significance to the person, a discussion of interesting aspects of employment, or a sincere expression of genuine esteem. Perhaps the most valid principle in helping a person come to a state of belonging is to be sensitive to and supportive of what is happening in the person's life.

The apostle Paul seemed to be aware of the need to reinforce and follow through in all Christian endeavor for he testified: "I have become everything . . . to men of every sort, so that in one way or another I may save some" (1 Cor. 9:22, NEB). If the apostle as an individual had this commitment to reinforcement activities, how much more a Sunday School and church must play their part in helping persons become fully assimilated and feel at home in the church. This wonderful end result is entirely worth the little effort required in reinforcing and reassuring a person as he grows into a genuine sense of oneness with his fellow Christians.

3. The Sunday School Establishes a Relational Dynamic

Human beings are instinctively relational. They have an intuitive urge to seek affinity and to search for reciprocity. This innate need for meaningful relationships is a part of man's divine endowment. It is one of the ways in which man is made in the image of God. Apparently God felt the desire to relate to beings similar to himself so he created Adam. He also made provision for Adam's need to relate by forming Eve from Adam's own body. From this remarkable beginning, interpersonal relationships have become the essential dynamic in human experience.

Relating to others is not only a human instinct and a human necessity, it also is an aspect of spiritual kinship. This fact lies behind a Christian's desire to relate to other Christians. It is also a basic motivation through which Christians seek to relate to non-Christians in an outreach framework. Sharing Christ is inherent in one's relationship to God.

The New Testament frequently illustrates the many vital relationships between fellow Christians and God. Although there were no perfect churches even in New Testament times, there are many examples of extremely significant experiences which grew out of their unique relationships.

The very word *assimilation* implies relationships. As a matter of fact, it implies a quality of relationship that is mutually acceptable and beneficial to all parties concerned. The word *assimilation* also speaks to the desirability of a relationship. For example, when a Sunday School unit *excludes* persons from its fellowship, by whatever means, it is saying "we do not wish to relate to you." Also, when a Sunday School unit *includes* a person it is saying, "We want to relate to you." In another more direct way, the act of assimilating new people is the most convincing way to communicate acceptance and to demonstrate the relational aspect of Christianity. On the other hand, failure to assimilate persons is the most convincing way to communicate rejection and prejudice and to demonstrate the very opposite of Christianity.

The Sunday School is the most useful means a church has for relating to new people so that assimilation of those persons can be achieved. Because the Sunday School structure is based on the age basis, it can provide the most direct and longest lasting relationships between a person and his peer group. Probably the full significance of peer grouping is rarely understood in its total scope. Peer relationships are the closest and most meaningful relationships. They often supersede parental and family relationships at least in terms of social enjoyment. This observation is based on the fact that peers relate on a time/culture pattern which is essential to compatibility. When peers use the terms "old-fashioned" and "newfangled," they are simply describing things or persons from their own time perspective.

Peer relationships are also highly significant in the developmental passages through life. This concept points up the mutuality of experiences which bind persons to each other and to their time culture. This is one reason why peers grow spiritually in their own groupings better than they do in the intergenerational environment.

Peer group relationships make a Sunday School class the most useful tool for the assimilation of persons into the church. The class in which one relates to his peers is the easiest place to be accepted, the best place to establish a base of interaction, and the most supportive group to which a member may relate. Because this relationship is stable and long lasting it is immeasurably important to both the member and the church as a whole. This significance of the Sunday School in appealing to the need to relate as an avenue for assimilation should strike a responsive chord for all church leaders. Far too many churches fail to sensitize their classes to their important role in assimilating new members. It is at the point of accepting and relating to new people that more good is achieved or more harm is done. This area of assimilation is almost the sole domain of the Sunday School, particularly the youth and adult divisions.

4. The Sunday School Maintains a Personal Support System

Nothing is more important in assimilating new members than the knowledge that they are being cared for, loved, ministered to, and supported by persons who have an empathetic understanding and a Christlike compassion for people. This need for a support system is actually bound up in the motivational forces of the psyche. It is generally expressed as a desire to be recognized although it may be incredibly disguised. In essence, the need for a support system is psychologically oriented. Thus it is best understood and serviced as a valid and wholesome desire as long as it is not compulsive or inordinate in its expression.

In the Christian context all forms of personal support are considered to be Christian ministries. The need for support is universal and the types of ministry are innumerable—as many as there are people—yet these ministries are basically contained in three categories: (1) spiritual ministries; (2) physical ministries; and (3) psychological ministries. From the spiritual viewpoint, ministry may be defined as an activity which expresses the love of Christ to other persons. In the physical sense, ministry is considered to be any activity which on Christ's behalf meets the physical needs of persons. And from the psychological stance, ministry is understood to be any activity which serves the cause of Christ with integrity. In all cases, ministry is a direct service for Christ and an indirect service to Christ.

A Sunday School class and department are excellent support groups for new members of the church. They serve in several ways to provide those things which cause new people to feel secure in a new situation. The fellowship, the meetings, the social activities, the visitation work, and the group ministry activities build spirit, generate warmth of heart, and provide necessary services to others. They also stimulate a depth of relationship between persons who participate. This result means that even the newest members should be involved in as many of these activities as possible. Because group activities involve persons they create a support system for all participants.

Acting as a support person can be a joyful ministry. It is a natural response to the specific needs of persons who have recently become Christ-folk. Because this ministry includes such things as physical assistance, psychological encouragement, material resources, and spiritual enlightenment, it is purely personal. This personal aspect of ministry is the sure road to self-acceptance, adequacy, and a growing feeling of being a vital part of something important. And these feelings are the evidence of one who both feels supported and who is in turn a supportive person. All of which is to say that assimilation is taking place.

5. The Sunday School Cultivates a Unique Fellowship

The New Testament describes a church from more than a dozen different perspectives. The apostle Paul used the term "body in Christ" (Rom. 12:5), to describe the functional roles of the corporate body as it manifests Christ in a given community. The church is also presented as a unique union of the divine object (God), and the human subject (man). In this sense the church is a *relational fellowship* of believers which is empowered by the Holy Spirit.

The word *fellowship* characterizes both the spirit and the bond between New Testament Christians. However, the word *fellowship* in the Scriptures is quite different from the common understanding of the word. *Fellowship,* in the popular concept, is generally equivalent to social fellowship. The Greek word translated *fellowship* is *koinonia.* It can be translated as *fellowship* as well as several other ways, yet it speaks primarily to a *relationship.* The relationship is one of cause and effect. Because a Christian is related to God through Christ, he or she is a child of God. This relationship to God brings him or her into a new relationship with other Christians because they become brothers and sisters in Christ. The spiritual union with Christ brings a spiritual kinship with other Christians. This is *koinonia.* In genuine *koinonia* there is an *upward* relationship to God and an *outward* relationship to fellow believers. Involved in both of these relationships there is a responsibility for those who are not yet in the *koinonia.*

This theological concept is beautifully expressed in the organized life of the church. For example, the vertical aspect of the *koinonia* relationship, or the man-to-God fellowship, is experienced in the corporate worship service. The horizontal aspect of *koinonia,* or the man-to-man fellowship, is experienced in the small-group experiences of the Sunday School. It is in this peer group relationship that the Christian community is best realized. In this setting persons *share* their common experience in Christ, *participate* in various aspects of their mission in Christ, and *celebrate* their partnership in the church of Christ.

It should always be remembered that the sharing and participating aspects of *koinonia* come before celebrating. When celebration is emphasized out of proper proportion it becomes just social fellowship. Under this condition, social fellowship becomes the goal rather than the result of *koinonia.* As the group moves away from the fellowship of the Spirit, it moves closer to the fellowship of man alone. At that point the group becomes a clique of man rather than a fellowship of the Spirit. As a consequence, it is no longer genuine and it tends to become an exclusive group rather than an inclusive fellowship. The integrity of the group becomes suspect when the group begins to lose interest in unreached persons. An authentic *koinonia* moves *outward* to unreached persons, but the spurious fellowship moves *inward* toward each other.

Although an authentic *koinonia* is expressed in many ways, it grows best when it is focused on teaching and learning the Scriptures. It is noted of the converts at Pentecost that they "continued steadfastly in the apostles' doctrine [teaching]" (Acts 2:42). This passage refers to the fellowship of learning. It was a direct response to the directive given in the Great Commission. Learning is the handmaid of personal growth and the source of highly significant fellowship. In this first formal approach to Christian growth and fellowship the new Christians were being taught, assured, encouraged, exhorted, strengthened, admonished, and firmly established in the faith.

While there is no specific information concerning the exact content of the teaching and learning in this first fellowship of growth, it is quite possible that the material now found in the four Gospels was the essence of that first Christian curriculum. Beyond any doubt a study and interpretation of the Old Testament Scriptures were also a part of the course.

The quality of the *koinonia* involved in this superb learning experience is rather obvious. There was a fellowship between the apostles as they planned, taught, and, no doubt, evaluated the process. There was a fellowship between the new converts as they examined their faith and shared their experiences. There was also an interlocking fellowship between the apostles and their class members as they came to know each other in Christ, experienced the edification process, and grew toward the maturity that is in the knowledge of Christ. There was also a fellowship with the Holy Spirit as they responded to his leadership in the process of learning. It was the Spirit who illumined their minds, encouraged their hearts, and filled their spirits to overflowing. It was no wonder that they were all experiencing a sense of awe. They were caught up in the *koinonia* of the Holy Spirit. That was a *koinonia* experience in its purest form.

The only comparable experience is that which can be enjoyed in a good Sunday School class. When a godly teacher, who is fully prepared, guides a compatible group of learners who are eager to participate in a meaningful search of the Scriptures, *koinonia* is experienced. This wonderful form of Christian accord may not be perfect, it would not be professional, it should not be academic, but it would be totally authentic. Furthermore, it would be singularly successful in doing just what Jesus himself did—communicating the gospel, bringing persons to salvation, and equipping Christians for the work of ministry.

Wrapping It Up

Churches live or die for a variety of reasons. Nevertheless, it is God's will that every church should not only live but grow. Those churches which die are probably those which fail to follow the biblical patterns of growth or lack the will to live.

Actually the Bible does not lay down rules for church growth, nor does it delineate any principles of church growth. However, it does record the specific growth activities of numerous churches and from these records certain concepts and practices are evident. When these concepts and practices are followed today, churches experience growth and vitality. Sometimes their growth is all but phenomenal.

It is a self-evident truth that present-day churches need to program biblical concepts in an appropriate and consistent fashion.

The basic biblical concepts of church growth may be stated in contemporary terms as follows:

1. The *overarching goal* in church growth is *making disciples.*
2. The *unique strategy* in church growth is *reaching unsaved adults.*

3. The *distinctive method* in church growth is *using the Sunday School.*
4. The *primary process* in church growth is *community outreach.*
5. The *essential activity* in church growth is *Bible teaching.*
6. The *basic technique* in church growth is *winning the lost.*
7. The *vital element* in church growth is *assimilating the converts.*

These concepts constitute a comprehensive view of church growth. When they are faithfully practiced, they generate church growth on a continuing basis. Furthermore, they will keep a church *focused on its mission,* for they are the very *essence* of Christianity!